GHOST SHIPS, GALES AND FORGOTTEN TALES

True Adventures of the Great Lakes

by Wes Oleszewski

Avery Color Studios

Gwinn, Michigan 49841

1995

GHOST SHIPS, GALES AND FORGOTTEN TALES

True Adventures on the Great Lakes

by Wes Oleszewski

Copyright 1995
by Avery Color Studios
Reprinted 1996, 1997, 1998

ISBN # 932212-83-2
Library of Congress Card # 95-079791

Published
by Avery Color Studios
Gwinn, Michigan 49841

*When Read Well —
Return To:
Gruesome
Grossman*

Dedication

To Ralph Roberts

A private, premier collector of all things nautical and relating to the Great Lakes, Ralph's bevy of information and documents is surpassed only by his passion for the gathering of such material. His insistence on keeping the facts straight is an example that all historians should follow and I often find myself asking if the tales that I have reconstructed can stand up to the "Ralph Roberts test," since he was reviewing Great Lakes history before I was born. With a common ground of both aviation and Great Lakes worlds, I am proud to say that Ralph has become my friend.

When Read Well –
Return to:

Table of Contents

Glossary

ABEAM—Directly beside a vessel

AFT—Toward the rear of a vessel

BACK—A ship's spine or keel

BARGE—A vessel that has no power of its own and must be towed

BEAM—The width of a vessel

BEAM ENDS—The sides of a vessel

BOAT—On the great lakes, a ship is called a boat

BULKHEAD—A wall-like partition that divides a boat's hull

BUNKER—A compartment where a boat's fuel is stored

CAPSTAN—Device used for pulling lines or chains

FIREHOLD—The part of the engine room where the boiler fires are fed

FO'C'SLE—The raised part of a boat's bow containing crew quarters

FOUNDER—To sink in a disastrous way

FUNNEL—A steamer's smokestack

HAWSER—A tow line, steel or rope

HEEL—To lean to one side

KEEL—A supporting beam that runs the length of a boat's bottom

LIST—A tilt to one side

LIGHTER—To raise a sunken boat by removing its cargo

PORT SIDE—Left side

SALTIE—An ocean going vessel that visits the lakes

SCHOONER-BARGE—A sailing vessel that is usually towed

SCREW—Propeller

SPARDECK—The maindeck through which cargo is loaded

TEXAS DECK—The deck atop which the pilothouse is mounted

YAWL—A small rowboat or lifeboat

Introduction

This book was 110 years in the writing. Considering that all of the tales contained within are true and that the earliest story takes place in 1883, it took a century for the persons and vessels described within this text to play out the events reported. None of the stories contained within these pages are of fiction. Each is a narrative of an actual occurrence, the thrilling drama of the ordeal and the tragedy of the losses are real and need no exaggeration. As in my other books, "Stormy Seas," "Sounds of Disaster," and "Ice Water Museum" — the tales here will be of the obscure events that have been under reported, or forgotten altogether. In fact, I feel that the more obscure the event, the better I like it. Not all of the stories involve the disastrous loss of lives and vessels, because often in the conflict between mankind and the Great Lakes, mankind wins.

When looking out across any of the Great Lakes, the shore-bound observer may be lucky enough to see the silhouette of one of the giant modern oreboats snailing upon the distant horizon. The courses and routes that these contemporary monsters follow are by no means new. In fact, they have been well traveled by countless mariners for more than a century and a half. Until very recently, lakers numbering in the hundreds marched along the horizons of the lakes from April until December. In the mid 1800s, it was often difficult to look toward the lakes from any single spot and see less than a half dozen distant boats at any time. Each of these vessels had a crew and each crewperson had a job to do and sometimes while just doing their jobs, these ordinary people found themselves cast into adventures that deserve telling. This book will attempt to do just that.

The information used in the production of the narratives that make up this text came from many sources. Often old newspapers were used to reference happenings, and there were the eyewitness accounts that came from interviews with individuals on the scene, or statements from research divers who have been down on the hulks of sunken lakers. There are the official records of vessels and the fabulous books of Great Lakes history written by other authors with the same interest as myself. And finally — there is ordinary circumstantial evidence.

You go to bed on a winter night and there is no snow on the ground, but when you wake the following morning there is four inches of snow. Although it may not be snowing at the time it is safe to say that during the night it snowed. Thus, if a vessel is running through a Lake Superior blizzard in late November, although nobody ever recorded the fact, it is safe to say that the crewmembers on deck were cold. This is circumstantial reasoning. In some cases, such circumstantial deduction was used to connect recorded facts in a logical flow. When printed quotes of dialogue were found it was used as factual conversation, but occasionally dialogue was synthesized to add a bit of texture to the narratives. Still there are no end of headaches in the interpretation of the facts available, but in every case this author has taken minimal liberties and made great efforts to keep the stories true.

A good example of some of the problems in interpreting the information at hand would be in the writing of the wreck of the J.L. CRANE. The newspaper report in the Sault Saint Marie Evening News stated flatly that the captain of the barge was named "Richard Griggs," but the Bay City Times Press named the luckless master as R. B. Briggs. Considering that the boat and its parent company were based in Bay City, I elected to use the Bay City Times Press name, as no other reference to the master's name could be found at the time of the writing. Later, Dr. Julius Wolff's outstanding book "Lake Superior Shipwrecks" was added to my personal library and he named the captain as Richard Briggs, citing the Duluth News-Tribune, and that is the way that the lost captain's name appears within this text. Additionally, the Evening News stated that snow accompanied the storm, but when I interviewed the eye witness to the sinking, he insisted that the night was "clear as a bell." Needless to say, that article in the Soo paper had to be taken with a grain of salt. On the other hand, there are a series of news stories describing the finding of the CRANE about a week after the sinking, but the eye witness claimed that he had never heard any story of the boat being found.

When writing of the W.P. THEW, many of the contemporary sources had her bound for "Alpena," but her carcass rests almost due east of the Thunder Bay Island light, well north and far to the east of a vessel bound for Alpena from Bay City. Since she had been shuttling limestone, her position led me to conclude that she was actually bound for Rogers City. At the time, Rogers City was a small village and the down-state papers would have used the much more familiar port of Alpena for expediency.

This all is a classic example of the struggle to take a few meager facts and by interpolating between them to come up with the most accurate chain of events possible to write the narrative. It sounds like a lot of toil over minute details, but that is what this kind of writing is all about.

There will always be as many ways to tell a story as there are story tellers, and this is particularly true in the telling of tales of the lakes. Whenever research divers find a long-lost wreck or whenever a dry land researcher spools a roll of microfilm at some out-of-the-way library, new facts are stumbled upon. These facts unfortunately often come to light after texts such as this have appeared at the bookstore. This is about two or more years too late for me to make changes and if I were to wait around for new discoveries the text would never come to print at all.

And there are the plain old mistakes that, when dealing with a text of greater than 60,000 words, we are all prone to make (think back to high school when you were asked to write an essay of 100 words, 1/600th of what you have here, and how hard it was to get it perfect). I do not claim that this text is perfection by any stretch of the imagination, and certainly there will be those who pick my work apart, event by event. As always this book is presented to you the reader to pick apart, double check, reference, ponder but most importantly to read and enjoy in any way you wish. I ask only that you know I have done my best to get it right.

Whalebacks and
Robber-Barons

*A*t the far western end of Lake Superior are the bustling ports of Duluth, Minnesota and Superior, Wisconsin, both of which have been the axis of the Great Lakes maritime industry since the mid-1880s. Giant lake freighters enter and depart through the natural harbor passage on the Superior side and the man-made ship canal on the Duluth side, departing with grain and iron ore. The harbor itself is a 24 mile long stretch of protected water that is bordered on the east by Minnesota Point and on the north and west by the majestic hills that rise as high as 800 feet. All of this serves well to shield the lakeboats and their crews from the spring and summer gales that frequent Lake Superior.

Up until 1871, only the natural entrance to the harbor at the Superior end was navigable and the citizens of Duluth soon began to feel the pinch. It was conceived to dig a canal through Minnesota Point so that vessels would not have to sail the seven odd miles from the port of Superior. The steam dredge ISHPEMING of the contracting firm of Dodge and Moses began the toil with craneman John H. Upham at the controls. All but one third of the distance to Lake Superior had been dug in late 1870 when that famous Duluth winter set in, freezing the ground and water glacier hard, so the work was stopped until spring. The spring thaw of 1871 brought Upham back to his rig and work on the canal charged ahead once more. No sooner had the steam shovels gone to work, than the municipality of Superior realized that there would be a financial loss, incurred by vessels bypassing their docks in order to sail directly into Duluth. This realization rolled through the halls of government like a clap of thunder and in a near panic, the Federal War Department was contacted by the Superior city fathers in an effort to get a court injunction to stop the canal's construction. It was the contention of those in Superior that a diversion of the St. Louis River, through the new canal, would shoal the Superior entrance and cut off the entire harbor while the Duluth people scooped at their ditch.

It did not take much to galvinize the War Department. On June 9th, 1871 a stop-work injunction was issued at Fort Leavenworth, Kansas and an army officer dispatched to serve the papers. Word of the impending federal action reached the populace of Duluth on a Friday evening, by telegraph. On the assumption that the U.S. Government does not do anything over a weekend, the citizenry took up shovels and began to dig by hand. Luckily, this was the era of Pony Express and not Federal Express, so Duluth Mayor J.B. Culver led a gang of more than 50 volunteers into an around-the-clock digging session. In the darkness of Saturday night, the rumble of dynamite was reportedly heard as the digging proceeded by torch light. By late Sunday, water flowed through the ditch, and with the level of the bay being slightly higher than the lake, nature was allowed to do the rest. As dawn broke on Monday, the federal Emissary was greeted by an opened 30-foot-wide canal, and the tug FERO steaming up and down tooting her whistle in defiant celebration. Standing among the piles of freshly-dug soil and rock with a limp court order in his hand, the federal man felt just a bit cheated. It is said that Canal Supervisor Munger pointed his finger at the new waterway. "You stop it if you can," he said bluntly to the federal man, "I can't." Each blast of the tug's steam whistle was an exclamation point to what everyone knew, that once opened the Duluth Ship Canal would never be closed. In the years that followed, the canal features were made permanent and the management of the waterway was taken over by the Army Corps of Engineers in 1873.

In modern times, when the lakers and salties approach the Duluth canal each shipping season, the appropriate chart for the channel is spread out in the pilothouse and closely examined by the mariners. Just two miles off shore and a few hundred feet south of the shipping lane, a high spot is indicated on the charts and marked as "Wk." Absolutely none of the vesselmen who pass that point pays the slightest consideration to the anonymous mark on the chart. After all, it has more than 50 feet of water over it and is well off of the steamer track. If they could only peer down through the depths, they would see the battered remains of what was once the finest product of the most creative mind on the Great Lakes. The silence of the wreck cloaks the jubilation that it once brought to the ports of Superior and Duluth as well as the horror.

On the first day of May, 1892, most of the communities around the Great Lakes were basking in the fresh breezes of spring as winter was being forgotten. However, at the head of the lakes the harbor waters of Superior, Wisconsin were still a jumble of broken ice. As usual, winter would be slow in releasing its grip on the port and spring was still a few weeks in the future. Crunching through the loose ice, looking like a giant floating cigar, another of Alexander McDougall's whaleback steamers rounded Conners Point and headed into the inner harbor. The rounded hull of the steamer sat high out of the water because she carried no cargo, her only burden today being a few dozen V.I.P.s that were aboard as guests of McDougall's American Steel Barge Company.

A fresh frosty breeze lofted through the pilothouse and found the back of Captain McArther's neck each time someone opened the door. All around the after deck, crowds of guests milled about and the scene seemed to be a mass of derby hats and dark overcoats. This was indeed a special day. It was the sea trials for the 320 foot steamer and everyone felt a special sense of excitement at being aboard the new steamer for her first taste of the lake. Captain McArther was given the honor of "bringing her out" and as he leaned against the window sill, he began making mental notes of each of the boat's unique wiggles. Atop her pilothouse the freshly-painted nameboard proudly displayed the whaleback's newly-christened designation, THOMAS WILSON.

Whalebacks as a breed were almost totally unique to the Great Lakes and were the product of the ingenuity of Captain McDougall. While sailing aboard his long-time friend Thomas Wilson's steamer HIAWATHA, and watching that boat's consort barges MINNIEHAHA and GOSHAWK trailing astern, McDougall brain-stormed of a barge that would be shaped in such a way as to follow the line of strain with the least resistance and least need for rudder. The barge would be cigar shaped with the exception of the sides and bottom which would be flat. The hull would be made of pre-fabricated iron plate and constructed on hoop-like ribs, making the cost of building the boat less than those of wood. In his mind's eye the captain saw that the seas washing over such a hull would, by their own weight, stabilize the hull. So as to offer a minimum of resistance to the seas, no cabins would be built upon the hull. Instead, large cylindrical turrets would support the deck houses and provide access to the lower portions of the hull via spiral stairways. The hatches would be hull plates that could be bolted down over a gasket so that they would not only be water-tight, but offer a minimum resistance to the seas. Continuing with the cigar shape, the bow and stern would curve upward to a blunt snout, with the hawsepipe for the tow line coming through there.

As soon as he could McDougall went to work making models of his idea. So encouraging were his results that he filed a patent on May 24th, 1881. More testing with models followed, and after 13 months he filed another patent, up-grading the original and considering the use of either iron or steel for the hull material. Now the captain turned inventor began to visit Great Lakes port cities in the hope of gaining financial backing for the construction of his newfangled boat. In the starched collar days of the 1880s such support for a man's vision was impossible to find. At one financial institution after another, McDougall was turned away. Sometimes, after listening to his proposal, the myopic bankers would politely turn him away, probably closing the door behind the inventor and scoffing to one another "A steel boat that rides mostly under the water? Nonsense!" and a chorus of deep chuckles they would go back to their bean counting. Many times the man with the cigar shaped boat was just plain thrown out. "You call that thing a boat," one particular banker growled, ". . . looks more like a pig!"

Interestingly, the first steel-hulled oreboat was the SPOKANE which came out in 1886. The fact that the vessel's hull was constructed of steel was simply due to a reduction of prices in that material, for originally it was to be made of iron, the fad of the era. McDougall had patented the idea of using steel for his whalebacks as early as four years before the SPOKANE's assembly. Captain McDougall's burden was that he was always ahead of his time and, perhaps, just a bit innocent as to the mind-set of the barons of business.

By 1887, McDougall had been turned down by every financial institution that he could think of. The old adage that says that the only time that you can get money from a bank is when you don't need it, held true. Finally Captain McDougall and his wife Emmeline invested all of their personal assets in the construction of his first whaleback at Duluth. Captain Thomas Wilson jumped in to aid McDougall and backed up his stated faith in the whalebacks with a substantial amount of his own money. Using local stevedores as laborers and shipping the bow and stern components from Wilmington, Delaware, McDougall launched barge 101 on the 23rd of June, 1888. Barge 101 performed exactly as advertised and the only variation from McDougall's patent appeared to be that the towing hawser came from the deck. Now the inventor looked toward a fleet of whalebacks, but again with no capital. At the urging of friends, Captain McDougall turned to the Rockefeller empire, and this time his brain-child was greeted with great interest by Rockefeller crony Colgate Hoyt. Soon a fleet of whaleback barges and steamers were on the way, as the American Steel Barge Company came to life.

When the first steamer came off the ways on June 9, 1890 it had the appearance of no powered freighter ever before seen on the lakes, and carried the name of Mr. Hoyt. With the same rounded lines of the barges, the steamers would have cabins perched atop the aft turrets. All of the accommodations, such as the pilothouse and officers quarters, would sit at the stern along with the engine works. The boat's smokestack had no rake and masts were an afterthought, McDougall's original design using masts only for elevating the running lights. Many vesselmen at the head of the lakes boasted that these boats were the wave of the future, but most mariners eyed the new boats with scornful suspicion. They dubbed the vessels "pig-boats" or simply "pigs," and the name stuck.

Production of the whalebacks proceeded at a wildfire pace, and just 17 months after the first steamer had been launched, the frames for the sixth steamer were put down. A dozen of McDougall's contraptions had already been launched, and his activities had outgrown the Duluth facility and been moved to Superior. The sixth steamer was laid out to be a true monster, measuring 320 feet in overall length and 38 feet in beam, and was assigned hull number 119. In less than six months, the largest whaleback ever built was ready for launching, named THOMAS WILSON after Captain McDougall's long time friend.

On the morning of April 30th, 1892 the WILSON was ready for her first taste of fresh water. McDougall's ship-yard superintendent and right hand man, Joseph Kidd had seen to it that all was in readiness for a spectacular launching. The slip that the WILSON would slide into was dredged a bit deeper than the normal eight to 13 feet, and lengthened to insure that the biggest whaleback would not scrape bottom. Around the yard red, white and blue banners and flags hung in decoration. Launchings in this era were a major celebration and the events ranged from high society lunches to drunken binges. Spectators were seated in viewing stands as if watching a great sporting event. At half past three in the afternoon, Superintendent Kidd gave the word and the blocks holding the WILSON back were sledged away, allowing the boat to slide down the 18 by 18 inch Washington fir launching skids. With a thunderous splash the massive hull plunged smoothly into the brackish water of the slip, bobbed like a rolling cork to one side and, with agonizing slowness, crashed into the piles of the opposite slip. For a moment the cheering stopped and was silenced in a startled gasp. That moment of hush was filled with the sounds of scaffolding crashing down, echoing across the festivities. Seconds later the newborn whaleback bounced playfully back into mid-slip without so much as a dent. The WILSON's impact had knocked down a part of the scaffold surrounding another whaleback under construction in the adjacent slip, but other than the man-hours needed to put the structure back together, there was no real damage. When the steamer was moored securely, she was opened to visitors and the celebration continued into the day.

Later that day steam was gotten up, and the basics for putting the WILSON in motion were arranged. Those lucky enough to tour the whaleback truly marvelled. Her cargo hold could swallow 3,300 gross tons of ore while drawing just over 16 feet of water. This the marine engineers had equated to a whopping 100,000 bushels of grain, all of which was far beyond the capacity of any other whaleback. She had 12 hatches measuring nine by 16 feet and spaced on 24 foot centers through which the cargos would be handled, while below her decks a powerful triple expansion engine hissed into life. Constructed at the Frontier Iron Works in Detroit, the engine provided 900 horse power at 92 revolutions, enough to allow the steamer to pull as many as three whaleback barges. Two Scotch boilers, measuring 10 feet nine inches by 13 feet and heated by six furnaces, provided the steam for the engine. The WILSON was surely the grandest whaleback ever constructed, but still the local media disdainfully described her as ". . . the biggest pig yet turned out."

A day after her launching the WILSON, garnished with her complement of guests, made her sea trial and two days later was formally turned over to the American Steel Barge Company. For the better part of the next week she was fitted with all of the appliances needed to put her and her crew to work, and finally tugged over to the Duluth side of the port and made fast below Elevator D. 90,000 bushels of grain were dumped into the hold and she headed off under Captain McArther for a Buffalo delivery.

In the same year that the WILSON was born, Captain McDougall was well on his way to making an empire of the

Crunching through the spring's harbor ice, the whaleback THOMAS WILSON heads out for sea-trials the day after her launching. Although their names are not listed on this photo, a careful look may identify the faces of such Great Lakes Legends as Alexander McDougall, Thomas Wilson and members of the Merritt clan among the deck load of V.I.P.s.

lakeboat business. The acquaintance of the whaleback inventor and Leonidas Merritt led to a contract that was supposed to cement McDougall's place at the top of the iron ore industry for the next decade and a half. Northwest of Duluth, the Merritt clan had opened the Mesabi Range of open pit ore mines, and that method of mining was far cheaper than the shaft method currently in use. The problem was that the Mesabi ore was quite powdery and tended to be blown out the stacks of the blast furnaces, so the steel companies considered it almost worthless. Mesabi ore had a very low price on the market place and because of this, railroads in the vicinity of the mines could not be tempted to lay down rails for carrying the red powder to the ore docks.

Undaunted, the Merritts started work on their own railway and announced that they would also build their own docks, but soon their precarious financing began to wear thin. McDougall, knowing that work was under way to modify the blast furnaces of the lower lakes to take Mesabi ore, contracted for his American Steel Barge Company to haul the Merritt powder until 1907. The contract also agreed to provide railroads and docks for handling the ore. The far-sighted McDougall knew that the nation's appetite for steel would not soon fade, and he was going to build a fleet of whalebacks dedicated to carrying Mesabi ore. In 1892, there were 10 whalebacks launched at McDougall's yard, a passenger boat, three barges and six steamers including the WILSON. Much of the WILSON's early career would surely be spent hauling Merritt ore.

When the financial panic of 1893 occurred, the whaleback steamer THOMAS WILSON did not know she was simply a machine. The people involved in her industry, however, found a turmoil that none of them could have predicted. From the east the Rockefeller empire sent corporate hatchet man Frederick T. Gates to the head of the lakes, to see to their best interest. In short order, the Merritts as well as Captain McDougall discovered the folly of doing business with Wall Street wolves. Taking advantage of Colgate Hoyt's recuperation from typhoid in Europe, Gates cancelled McDougall's 15 year hauling contract with the Merritts, who were yet to complete the rail lines from their mines. He removed the Merritts from management of the company that owned the mines and railroads, and attempted to drive a stake between them and McDougall by offering the captain that job. McDougall refused. Next Gates attempted to mix Captain McDougall into a personal squabble with Gates' rival Hoyt. Again McDougall refused. Finally, like any good corporate raider, Gates turned to contractual games and Captain McDougall, like the Merritts, found himself losing everything, including his whaleback patents. When it was all over the whaleback maker was offered the General Manager's position and dejectedly accepted. The production of whalebacks ground to a halt, but the WILSON sailed on. Needless to say, there were no statues erected in honor of Frederick Gates at the head of the lakes.

Often towing whaleback barges, the WILSON sailed under the American Steel Barge Company until the opening of navigation in 1900. On the 22nd day of March that year, she was placed into Rockefeller's Bessemer Steamship Company, along with all but eight of seven of the existing whalebacks. The eighth missing member of the fleet was barge 115, which had gone to the bottom of Lake Superior the previous December. This move was an effort to keep the members of the American Steel Barge Company from falling prey to the rapidly-forming Pittsburgh Steamship Company. The full reasoning behind the merger will probably never be known to anyone except the turn of the century robber-barons, because a year later the whole of the Bessemer Fleet was sold to those same Pittsburgh interests. With that, the WILSON made her final change of ownership.

The opening of the 1902 season found the majority of the whalebacks wearing the colors of the Pittsburgh fleet, hulls painted a rust brown, with white cabins and a stack painted silver. This fleet, that would at one point number more than 100 vessels, clamped a near monopoly on the movement of ore across the lakes and was thus dubbed "the steel trust." Like her sisters, the WILSON crushed through the spring ice wearing a tin-colored stack and normally with one of Captain McDougall's barges strung to her stern. Ironically the whalebacks often carried the powdery ore from the Mesabi Range, ore discovered and first developed by the Merritt family, who had faded into obscure poverty.

Dawn on the seventh day of June of that same year illuminated the low squatting hull of the WILSON, moored to the Mesabi ore dock. Through the night there had been the normal hodgepodge of loading delays that have always been a part of the maritime industry, so by daylight the whaleback's master, M.C. Cameron, found himself considerably behind schedule. It appeared that the last of the ore would come down the shoots just after breakfast, so the captain left orders that as soon as the shoots started to clear, the lines were to be cast off. Considering that Lake Superior was flat calm, the hatches would be set down and sealed after the boat cleared Duluth. Whaleback hatches, being a part of the hull plating, needed to be set by hand and were very difficult to manipulate. Loitering at the dock while the crew man-handled the hatches could delay the WILSON's departure well into the afternoon. When the last trickling of ore dropped into the hold, Captain Cameron gave a tug on the whistle-pull and the lines were unlooped from the bollards.

Amidst billows of thick black coal smoke, the whaleback's stern pulled from the dock as she churned in reverse. At the wheel Milo Banker spun the spokes to the commands of the captain, while John Campbell, the watchman, peered over the rail to insure that the steel cigar cleared the other boats crowding the slip. As the boat cleared the dock and reached the open bay the captain rang "Ahead full," and ordered the boat hard-over on the right wheel. Looking more like a surfaced submarine than an oreboat, the WILSON pointed her snout toward Conners Point and the Duluth ship canal. It was just before 10 o'clock that Saturday morning and the whaleback's cargo was destined for South Chicago. Oddly, the WILSON was running without her normal consort barge to further burden her. Considering this, Captain Cameron figured that they would make the Soo at about four o'clock the next afternoon. If they did not run into the normal traffic jam at the locks, they should pull up under the unloading rigs at South Chicago just before dawn Tuesday.

As the WILSON snored toward the narrow passage of the ship canal, the tug ANNIE L. SMITH was just ahead— also steaming toward the open lake. The tug was going out to meet the 296 foot wooden steamer GEORGE G. HADLEY, inbound and still a couple of miles out on the lake. This was an era long before the creation of the marine radio telephone, so the tugs were normally sent out carrying changes of orders such as dock or cargo alterations. This morning the message was for the HADLEY to take her coal cargo through the Superior entrance rather than the Duluth canal. In modern times this whole process seems very inefficient, but in 1902 it was all in a day's work.

There was no need for the WILSON to check her speed as the tug was pulling away, so Captain Cameron just "kept her comin.' " The city of Duluth drifted by as the whaleback was lined up between the newly-constructed piers. The canal was at the end of a lengthy construction effort to modernize the passage, in fact the south pier had been finished since 1900 and the final touches were being applied to the north pier.

Below the WILSON's forward turret, in his fo'c'sle cabin, fireman E.H. Shoemaker was just crawling into his bed for a few hours of sleep. His previous shift had been an easy one as he had only to shovel enough coal to keep steam alive in the boilers. The next shift, with the WILSON fully loaded and bound across Lake Superior would be far more work, so a nap was definitely in order. Cabins below decks in the whalebacks were dark, damp and stuffy with no portholes. Fresh air was available only through vents that extended above the turrets, and light came from a dim oil lamp or a dismal light bulb. The boats were not designed with human comfort in mind, so sleeping was an acquired skill. No matter, a bunk away Shoemaker's room-mate Sam Conors was sound asleep.

Aft in the galley Adron Tripp, the cook, was getting a start on lunch while Guy Frink, the second cook, was putting up the last of the breakfast dishes as outside of the windows the cement walls of the ship canal passed silently. Second Mate Neil McGilvray stepped to the rail in front of the pilothouse, Lake Superior was a breathtaking sky-blue and as flat as plateglass. Before going down on deck to tend to his routine he would pause for a while and soak up as much of the fresh air as he could. Ashore, there were plenty of boat-buffs passing Saturday morning watching the comings and goings of the lakers with their everpresent binoculars. Across the sapphire distance they saw the tug SMITH easing up to the HADLEY and the WIL-SON coming along to pass. The whole scene was like a painting.

Mate McGilvray came down the ladder to the spar deck as the WILSON started to pass the HADLEY. Strolling past the yawning hatches he figured that he would check the forward equipment first, then muster up the boys to close the hatchcovers. He had gotten to midships when the deck abruptly lurched beneath his feet, as if the boat were rolling steeply in abeam sea. There was a thunderous deafening rumble and the mate was nearly knocked from his feet as he stumbled into the fence wires. Regaining his balance a bit his attention was immediately drawn to the cause of the jolt. The bluff bow of the HADLEY was impacted deeply into the hull of the whaleback, just ahead of the aftermost hatch, and was shoving her over steeply to starboard. Before his heart beat a few times more, the WILSON recoiled back to port, sharply slamming down on the HADLEY's prow. Instantly the second mate knew that his boat was doomed and that he had to alert the others, if the collision had not already done that. As if in a nightmare, he ran aft to the open companionway and shouted down that the boat was sinking, then charged up the ladders to the deck house roof where the lifeboats were stored. His pulse rapidly pounding at his ears, McGilvray reached the lifeboats—and found himself completely alone. Huffing breaths of terror, the mate looked around in wide-eyed astonishment. The lifeboats could not be launched by one man alone. He was helpless.

In the fo'c'sle, the jolt had gotten the attention of Fireman Shoemaker, to say the least. Shoemaker was the survivor of four previous shipwrecks, and knew all too well the implications of the radical movement of a deck beneath him. Clad only in a shirt and undershorts he dashed to the stairway and climbed to the deck level. A single glance aft said it all and Shoemaker scrambled back to his room and woke his roommate, still sound asleep. Again the fireman bounded on deck and started aft toward the lifeboats. He had made only a stride when the WILSON made her recoil to port, forcing him to go hand-over-hand along the starboard fence. Figuring the whaleback might plunge beneath him, Shoemaker simply leaped overboard and started swimming for all he was worth.

From the WILSON's pilothouse Captain Cameron was unable to believe his eyes. The whole mess had started as he neared the HADLEY and saw her turning in his direc-

Beached just outside of Duluth, the GEORGE G. HADLEY appears at her end. Not far astern, the THOMAS WILSON rests below the waves—forever.

tion as if to pass behind the whaleback and head for the Superior entrance. Continuing along his course, the whaleback's master brought her across the turning steamer's bow. Just when it looked like the HADLEY would scrape clear astern, the wooden steamer swung suddenly to port and smashed into the WILSON. In that instant, the WILSON's master realized the folly of leaving the dock without his hatches being sealed. With nothing to keep air pressure in her cargo hold, the boat would sink like a bathtub with a hole axed in its side.

Wheelsman Banker threw the wheel hard over and both he and the captain headed for the lifeboats. Unfortunately, they neglected to ring "stop" on the engine chadburn before they vacated the pilothouse. Everywhere on deck the scene was of men stripping what clothes they could and jumping into Lake Superior. The WILSON was sinking nose first and at a shocking pace. When they reached the lifeboats they found the befuddled second mate slashing at the life raft stays with his knife. He was joined by watchman Campbell who, only a moment earlier, had been attempting in vain to pull his rubber boots off in anticipation of an inevitable swim. Judging that launching the life raft was useless, the wheelsman decided that his chances were better with the lake and leaped for his life. Stepping to the aft rail, Captain Cameron witnessed a mammoth blast of steam bursting through the companionway doors from below, as the frigid lake found the red-hot boilers. The explosive mixing of the two made a roar as the stern of the whaleback rose up under the captain's feet and the steam came up and swallowed him whole. Like a boulder the whaleback plunged to the bottom of Lake Superior, with her propeller still whirling at full ahead.

Clawing and kicking at the icy blackness that surrounded him, Captain Cameron struggled amidst a thousand swirling currents as he was pulled toward the depths of Superior. Ice water blocked his ears and shot up his nose as he tumbled helplessly with the eddies. One of his hands struck out and he touched someone else thrashing near—an instant later the drowning master was alone once more. After what seemed like an eternity, he burst through the surface, choking and gasping in a jumble of jagged flotsam.

Near to where the captain surfaced, the second mate popped up, coughing for a single breath. The current left by the whaleback's screw pushed the survivors and wreckage aft toward the HADLEY. Frantically, McGilvray gathered any pieces of wreckage that might buoy him up when, like the answer to a prayer, he floundered smack into the WILSON's life raft. The raft, simply four drums fastened to a wooden lattice, had apparently ripped free as the whaleback went down. The lucky mate pulled himself aboard and took a second to catch his breath. He was drifting close to the HADLEY when his attention was drawn to a chorus of calls in the distance. "Save the captain!" the voices shouted, "Somebody get the captain!" Looking around, McGilvray spotted Captain Cameron, near exhaustion, a short distance from the raft. At that same moment one of the HADLEY's firemen called out and tossed McGilvray an oar, which he promptly put to work, pulling the shaken captain to safety.

A frenzy of tossing anything that would float from the HADLEY took place as one by one those lucky enough to have gotten away from the whaleback swam to safety. Fireman Shoemaker, the shipwreck veteran, got to the HADLEY and scaled right up the wooden steamer's oak bow timbers like a monkey. When the HADLEY's wheelsman, Fred Briffin, saw him sloshing across the deck in his underwear, he directed the born survivor below decks, where he could find a spare set of overalls. Shoemaker had now been through five shipwrecks. Not so lucky were the staff of the whaleback's galley. Cook Tripp was spotted going down for the last time and slipped below the lake as floatable devices splashed nearby. The second cook was simply missing from the wreck mayhem, never to be seen again. John Campbell, the watchman who tried to help the mate free the raft, never surfaced. Perhaps he was the man that the captain touched in his own struggle to surface. Thomas Jones and John Carey, both deck hands, did not find safety and were swallowed by Superior as was wheelsman Joseph McGraw. Three of the WILSON's engine crew, James McDougall and James McFraser were taken by the lake, as was fireman William Roebuck. Nine of the whaleback's crew died with her.

Before long the WILSON's captain and mate were plucked from the life raft and taken aboard the tug SMITH, then transferred to the HADLEY. When he was sure that no one alive was still in the water, Captain Fitzgerald, the HADLEY's master, started tending to his own boat. A hurried inspection showed the boat's timbers to be holding with only a trickle of Lake Superior intruding. In fact the captain was so secure in the HADLEY's seaworthiness that he elected to get up steam and head for the Superior entrance to the harbor, some six miles south of the collision site. Considering that the Duluth entrance was only half that distance, Captain Fitzgerald's decision to head south showed real confidence in his boat's condition. It was his second major miscalculation of the morning. No sooner was the HADLEY well underway than she began to flood rapidly and in a matter of minutes it appeared that she was about to join the WILSON on the bottom.

Realizing the folly of his decision Captain Fitzgerald ordered the HADLEY turned back for the Duluth canal, but the boat filled even more rapidly. It is not difficult to imagine the feelings of the WILSON's survivors, since it appeared they would soon be swimming again. Alarmed by the HADLEY's rate of settling, the captain ordered the boat headed to the shallows, just south of the Duluth canal wall. The incoming lake was threatening the fires and the engine room began to flood. Chief Engineer John Hogan ordered the fire hold crew up on deck, in case the cold lake should hit the boilers, causing an explosion that would kill every one below decks. Hogan would nurse his beloved engine works alone—come what may. Filthy choking steam saturated the surrounding air, as the fire hold flooded and the HADLEY foundered. The chief felt the HADLEY's engine room floor grating shudder beneath his feet, and knew at once that she had been beached. Wading to the companionway, Chief Hogan half swam out of the engine room, then bounded up on deck. Using the emergency release valve, he let go the steam from the boilers.

No sooner had the HADLEY beached than she sank by the stern, all the way up to the roof of her aft deck house.

By mid-afternoon everyone had been removed from the HADLEY, and fireman E.H. Shoemaker had survived his sixth shipwreck overall . . . and his second in just one day.

A small tug hovered over the WILSON's grave, 17 days after she went to the bottom. Over the side splashed a hard-hat diver and slowly sank down. After a length of time the diver gave the yank on his tether and was brought back to the surface. The crew gathered near as the diver's brass helmet was removed, "So, how's she look?" the salvage captain inquired. "It must be in 70 feet," the diver explained, "cus the deck's at about 50. There's a big "V" gash in the port side just ahead of the forward turret, with a crack right in one of the seams runnin' across the deck to about a foot and a half of the starboard fence. The hole in her side is so big you can see ore comin' out. All her hatches are off too. It's really murky down there and you can't see more than a few feet." As he listened to the diver's report, the salvage captain knew deep down that there was no real chance of bringing up any part of the WILSON. If anyone should know about whalebacks it was this captain. His name was Joseph Kidd, the once omnipresent superintendent of McDougall's whaleback yard—who had given the signal to launch the THOMAS WILSON a decade earlier.

Over the years that followed the WILSON's sinking there were many who thought they knew better than Joseph Kidd and that the severed whaleback could be raised. Half-hearted efforts continued as late as the early 1960s, but the WILSON remained firmly stuck in Superior's bottom. When the Duluth harbor was dredged, the spoils were dumped right on the resting whaleback. Today, the WILSON is so forgotten that her grave has been designated as an anchorage for salt water vessels. Their giant steel hooks are often dropped directly on the once grand whaleback, pummeling this historic treasure. It is a sad, slow demolition of what was once celebrated as the pinnacle of her kind.

Whalebacks in general never did appear in the masses that it was once thought that they would. It was found that the "true" whaleback design could not be practical at lengths beyond 405 feet and by the mid 1890s steel lakers were already pushing beyond those dimensions. Too, the new Hulett unloaders on the lower lakes could not effectively work through the whaleback's narrow hatches. Frederick Gates' shenanigans and the 1893 panic did not help in the evolution of the whalebacks either. Had McDougall been left alone he might have produced whalebacks in such numbers that it would have forced the development of unloading equipment more suitable to their design. This was not to be. By 1906 the fleet of McDougall's whalebacks was approaching extinction on the Great Lakes as their numbers were being shifted to salt water service.

Alexander McDougall and Leonidas Merritt were good people of the Great Lakes, with mid-western ethics as basic as the earth from which their ore was mined. Their only shortcoming was in trusting those from the east coast who valued numbers in a ledger more than people. Time, however, has a way of evening the score in one way or another. Today, the last intact whaleback is the museum ship METEOR, which is permanently on display for the public to visit at Barkers Island, at the port of Superior. Alexander McDougall is a legend on the Great Lakes and Frederick Gates has been appropriately forgotten. Captain Cameron had his master's certificate suspended for a mere 60 days, probably for failing to blow passing signals and, or check down while passing. On the other hand, Captain Fitzgerald of the HADLEY had his papers revoked permanently for his part in the WILSON's end. Fireman Shoemaker earned the bragging rights as the man who had survived the most shipwrecks in Great Lakes history, and he was probably right. Rockefeller's monopoly fleet of more than 100 vessels has dwindled to 10 and those are directed by faceless off-lakes interests as a small sideline of their global shipping operations. And lastly, Leonidas Merritt and his kin—just like the THOMAS WILSON, and their brief star-crossed, yet *important* place in Great Lakes history—faded away and were all but forgotten. To most reading this tale, the remains of hull 119, located at the far western tip of Lake Superior, are as distant as the events themselves. Perhaps now, however, the lost whale-back is more than just a mark on a chart.

Setting the Record Straight

*W*ithin the second half of the 1800s, there occurred an explosion in commerce on the Great Lakes. Crowds of lakeboats, small, large and in between made their living hauling anything that would fit into their holds. Vessels of sail and steam alike were found milling about the crowded freshwater ports. During the 1860s and 70s it was a confusing time indeed, wooden vessels plopped from the ways of small independent shipyards, with little or no proclamation. Many times a vessel would be constructed by a private owner, to be managed by him and perhaps captained by him as well. In this, the era before big shipping lines, these one-man owner-operator vessels became traveling "small businesses." Often, as quickly as the lakers would be launched they would be pushed into obscurity by the coming out of a vessel of greater elegance or larger size, thus adding to the confusion of the period.

For decades the self-contained, floating small businesses tramped about the lakes seeking cargos of opportunity. At times, they would wait in port and engage a payload only when the price was considered to be worthwhile, or if the rates of cargo from the destination port looked ripe. Boats would head to a distant port simply on the rumor of profits to be earned. Such movement was often done without a word, as the knowledge of profitable cargos to be had would draw competing boats from all over the freshwater seas. It was better indeed to slip from Chicago and just show up at Bay City, in time to haul a shipment to Buffalo—before the notice of such intentions could draw a crowd of followers, all wanting a piece of the profits. From a historic perspective, the problem here was that the movement of these vessels normally went untracked and were noted only by obscure second-hand references. "The schooner such and such was seen passing such and such to-day and she is thought to be on the coal run for so and so," would be an apt paraphrase found in the marine column of a local newspaper, a day or two after the fact- of course. When one of these vessels was unlucky enough to meet her fate, the facts surrounding the vessel's end would fade as readily as the profits that she had once earned.

It was probably 1865 when the little steamer TRADER first found freshwater. Most believe that the birth occurred at the port city of Newport, Michigan, which that same year was renamed Marine City. Just over 15 years later, on October 18, 1880, the Lake Michigan surf cast up the promenade deck, wheel rope and large amounts of lumber identified as belonging to the TRADER. It was the day after one of the worst storms in Lake Michigan's history, a tempest that swallowed the big passenger sidewheeler ALPENA with all aboard. Dozens of other lakers were blasted from the lake's surface like feathers on a puddle when the mighty breath of the storm came booming. Schooners, steamers, barges and tugs were thrown indiscriminately against the nearest shore, by what was etched into Lake Michigan's history as the monstrous "Alpena storm." Now apparently, there was mute evidence that the blow had taken the little TRADER as well. The day following the wreckage's appearance, the Bay City Evening Press had picked up a telegraphic Associated Press dispatch from Chicago that attempted to detail the storm. Largely, the article told the latest of the ALPENA's disastrous loss, but mixed within the report was the following information:

"The steam-barge Trader, which plies between Chicago and Muskegon and does a lumber business, and which, according to advices and the reports of officers of schooners who have seen her wreck, has been lost and gone to pieces on the east shore of Lake Michigan, was captained by Frank Brown, and manned by a crew of 10." The story then went on to simply state the fate of those aboard by adding bluntly, "All hands have probably perished." This dispatch was flashed to nearly every newspaper around the lakes as a tragic sidelight to the growing fame of the "Alpena storm." As Captain Frank Brown ruffled through the pages of the Grand Rapids Daily Eagle, searching for information on the storm, he came upon the words of his own demise—and emitted a hefty "hurumph!"

"Lost with all hands," the gruff master of the TRADER snorted under his breath with disgust, "astonishing." Rolling the newspaper up and tucking it under his arm the annoyed captain turned his back to the blustery wind and headed up the street, blending into the townsfolk.

For the next 110 years this story of the TRADER's fatality hibernated within the yellowing copies of assorted local newspapers from Chicago to Duluth to Buffalo. At various times, some of those papers were transferred onto micro film and dispatched to local libraries. The little steamer's story, as well as the tales of many other lakers involved in the storm, was overlooked time and time again as authors and historians went sifting through the details of ALPENA's spectacular loss. Certainly the disappearance of the 643 ton, 170 foot sidewheel passenger steamer, with perhaps as many as 101 souls, was a tragedy that most writers and researchers could not resist, so it has over the years been well penned. But in doing so, they have seemed to overlook such vessels as the TRADER, GRANADA, MARY GROH, BRUNETTE and DAVID A. WELLS—until the preparation of this text.

The whole story begins as Indian summer was warming lower Lake Michigan on Friday, October 15th, 1880. A light southerly breeze ushered temperatures in the 60 degree range that topped as high as an unseasonable 70 degrees. Afternoon of that balmy autumn day would see the canal schooner DAVID A. WELLS tacking her way toward Chicago with a belly full of Escanaba iron ore. At that same time, across the lake to the east, at the port of Muskegon, the schooner GRANADA was taking aboard the last planks of a lumber cargo bound for the same port city as the WELLS. At South Haven, Michigan, the 120 foot rabbit steamer MARY GROH was also taking on a cargo bound for Chicago. Her hold was stuffed with 100 barrels of crisp Michigan apples, while a gang of lumber-shovers was stacking a load of fragrant lumber on the deck. Purchasing passage to the windy city aboard the GROH was a local fisherman, Henry Winsted, one of 15 persons who had paid to be aboard for a crossing that normally took about eight hours. In terms of 1880 modes of transportation, this was indeed an express passage, and such stand-up bookings on freighters bound from the southern Lake Michigan shore to Chicago were common. All around the lake, every vesselman was attempting to make the best of the mild weather to foster their floating "small businesses." They knew all too well that mother nature would not hold her temper forever. No force can stop the seasons from changing, and mid-way through October, it was a sure bet that fall and winter conditions were not far away.

As the sun sank into Lake Michigan, Captain Robert Linklater stood at the stern rail of the schooner GRANADA minding her wheel, as his brother Angus barked the standard commands for setting sail. With the Linklater brothers as its only officers, this boat was indeed a small family business. Among the rigging and masts, crewmen William Best, Owen Connelly, Michael Duffy and William Bissell worked like circus performers, as the boat found the lake breeze and heeled her way into the night. There were two additional members of the schooner's crew: one, a deck-hand whose name was recorded only as M. Lap, and the ship's cook whose identity has been obliterated by the passing of time, as it was never recorded at all. Angled into the growing southerly wind, the 229 ton wind-grabber was headed directly into the jaws of the worst storm in Lake Michigan's recorded history.

Tar-black was the night as the once balmy winds began to change into autumn bluster. Just before three o'clock on Saturday morning the wind practically exploded into a violent gale, as the temperature plummeted to sub-freezing. In less time than a sailor can scramble up a schooner's rigging, Indian summer turned into a freakish snow-hurricane so violent that witnesses thought they had been hit by a tornado. This storm, however, was far more massive than an isolated tornado—it swallowed Lake Michigan whole.

With no form of weather forecasting, scores of vessels and their people were caught on the open lake amid shrieking winds and rapidly-developing seas, their sails opened fully to the thundering tempest. Along the Michigan shore the winds were later reported as peaking at 80 miles per hour at Frankfort, 75 miles per hour at Ludington, 65 miles per hour at Charlevoix and 60 miles per hour at South Haven. Across all of Lake Michigan's surface, schooner crews scrambled among the standing rigging of their vessels in a desperate effort to set for the storm. Masters reached into the heaving night with their minds, attempting in desperation to plot their way to safe-ty through the blackened maelstrom. Among the desperate masters was Captain Linklater whose schooner GRANADA had been caught nearly half of the way across to Chicago. As the once mild lake turned into foam-capped hills of ice water roaring ahead of an arctic wind, the good captain came to the realization that he was in a bad spot.

Also ensnared on the exposed lake was the steamer MARY GROH, which had left South Haven late Friday evening. Steaming in a dead swell, the diminutive laker abruptly found herself beating into a howling blow. The boat's master had no choice other than to call for more steam, as the GROH was being effortlessly blown from her Chicago course by a mighty wind, the likes of which no one on lake Michigan had ever seen before. Blasting from due south, the storm had robbed all vessels of any kind of handy shelter. The GROH's master chose to simply head into the wind, and run from the surface of the lake toward any landfall. Gathering every ounce of mariner skill, the GROH's skipper turned his boat against Lake Michigan and commenced battle.

Elsewhere on the lake the struggle had already been decided. Shortly after the gale had pounced upon her, the GRANADA became unmanageable in the seas. Having been set to catch the earlier breeze and with the crew having no time to rig for the storm, the schooner's foresail and jib would have been early victims of the wind. Shortly after the sailor's had raised what storm rigging they could, the schooner inexplicably started to fall off into the trough of the sea. A quick inspection of the GRANADA's steering apparatus showed it to be undamaged, but ineffective. The trouble became obvious—the lake had bitten off the schooner's giant oak rudder and swallowed the steering vane as easily as a snack cracker. The canvas-powered laker was set upon by Lake Michigan's rage, stays snapped, storm sails shredded and masts cracked off, as the boat was pounded in the murderous sea trough. The whitecaps reached up and plucked the GRANADA's lifeboat like picking a ripe berry, marooning her crew to find their fate with their vessel.

When the gray dawn broke it appeared as if the GRANADA was about to go to pieces. Each wave twisted her hull, working the caulking from her butts and washing over the deck. Her deck cargo had gone over the side long before the belated daylight arrived, and now only the foaming seas traveled between the rails. The boat's quarters had been invaded and ravaged by the frigid lake and smashed by the shifting lumber cargo. Now the GRANADA's crew had been forced onto the open deck and were constantly being drenched by waves of the numbing lake.

Thick snow swirled with the whipping wind gusts, as the hours dragged by and the GRANADA began to make terrifying noises, the likes of which none of her crew had heard before. The ship's cook was near panic, fearing that each billowing wave held the doom of everyone on board. One of the crew went to calm the troubled cook and the two frightened sailors huddled together against the merciless lake. At noon Mate Angus Linklater noticed that neither the cook nor the compassionate crewman who went to settle him were moving, and he went to check on them. The cook's arms were black from frost-bite and both he and his nearby shipmate were dead. Taking some of the shredded canvas that had once been one of the GRANADA's sails, Mate Linklater wrapped the two corpses as best he could, too benumbed himself to feel his own hands and fingers, let alone much grief. Perhaps the two expired crewmen were a prelude to what was in store for all of the GRANADA's souls.

About the same time as the GRANADA appeared to be in her death throes, the MARY GROH was continuing to struggle with Lake Michigan. The little steamer was just a short distance from the beleaguered GRANADA, but the two were completely isolated from one another by a curtain of snow. Earlier that morning, the GROH's duel with the lake had turned significantly in the lake's favor. She had aboard enough fuel to make the trip to Chicago and back, but the explosive winds cut the steamer's forward speed to nothing, forcing the master to deplete his fuel bunkers in an effort to just keep the boat's head to the seas. Towering whitecaps boarded the little steam-barge, carrying away her deck load of lumber as if it were matchsticks. On deck, her crew did what they could to keep the vessel trimmed, but as they did, the seas came in an attempt to carry them off as well. Sometime during the ordeal, passenger Henry Winsted, the lake fisherman, was clutched by the waves and taken overboard to his doom. With his fuel and crew exhausted, the GROH's master had just one chance left to save his boat. Giving the order for the frostbitten crew to raise the steamer's lone storm-sail, at the steam-barge's forward mast, the captain brought the GROH around, with considerable difficulty, and sailed her with the wind up the Wisconsin shore. At 10 o'clock that morning while running before the wind, those aboard the GROH spotted the steamer ALPENA, wallowing in the seas about 10 miles off of Kenosha, Wisconsin in the company of the schooner S.A. IRISH. Soon the snow blotted out the two boats from the GROH's view. An hour later Captain Webber, of the IRISH, would turn for Milwaukee, leaving his parallel course with the ALPENA. Captain Webber and his crew would be the last people to see the ill-fated sidewheeler, as sometime thereafter the ALPENA went missing in the rampaging seas and the storm that would wear her name among Great Lakes lore.

About 150 miles up from where the GROH was pounding, the schooner-barge BRUNETTE had been left to her own ends by her tow. The boat's cargo of corn was being invaded by the lake, her seams leaking and her hull twisted, as she was tossed like a twig. Using every bit of skill that he could muster, her captain was attempting to guide the BRUNETTE into Bailey's Harbor. The storm blew out her fore and main sail and smashed her main boom. Amidst the clamor her captain was thrown against the cabin, breaking his leg. Perhaps Lake Michigan was preoccupied with swallowing the ALPENA—or maybe it was blind luck—but somehow the BRUNETTE managed to make the harbor's relative shelter and drop her hooks. Three feet of water sloshed among the BRUNETTE's cargo of corn, but compared to some others at Bailey's Harbor, she was well off. Against the pier the CITY OF CHICAGO sat wind-bound and unable, or perhaps unwilling, to depart. The schooner ALICE B. NORRIS pulled on her anchor chains as the waves slapped at her, the boat's mainsail, jib and fore gaff topsail split by the winds and her lifeboat and bulwarks carried off by the seas. Sulking in the harbor were the schooners THREE BELLS, ADA MADORA and CASCADE, each with foresail blown to rags, jib booms splintered, damaged mainsails and missing yawl boats. The schooners GUIDE, JAMES PIATTE, EAGLE WING and DELOS DE WOLFF were visible through the squalls of snow, holding at anchor and licking wounds similar to the others in the harbor. Among those sheltered, only the schooner SKYLARK was undamaged. What no one knew was that this was just one pocket of shelter on the Lake Michigan shore—every cove and bay was quickly crowded with fleeing vessels.

Most of the survivors of the "Alpena storm," believed that the blow peaked at about suppertime on Saturday, but the heavy snow and gale-force winds persisted through Sunday. Winds were estimated at 55 miles per hour and unbelievably seemed to hover there for nearly 48 hours—in some areas three feet of snow had accumulated and was still coming down. Through the seemingly endless night that divided Saturday from Sunday, the battered GRANADA drifted, wallowing in the sea trough. She was the sole thing left afloat on the uninhabitable open lake.

Her surface was caked with frozen slush and the crew shivered in drenched clothing, stiffened with cold. At noon Sunday, the benumbed crew sighted land through the snow squalls and a weakened cheer went up at the thought that soon their boat might find solid ground. Had the survivors of the GRANADA's crew been able to see three hours into their future, they would never have cheered at all.

The tender hull of the GRANADA, pushed by the southwesterly gale-force winds, slammed into the state of Michigan at half past two o'clock Sunday afternoon. Her jolt was violent—the towering surf dumped the nearly sunken hull into shallow water, a sizeable distance from the beach. Oddly, the GRANADA had fetched up just two miles from the place where she had started her ordeal a day and a half before, the port of Muskegon. Ashore, local residents had kept a sharp eye out for vessels in distress and had spotted the GRANADA long before she found the bottom. A small boat and a gaggle of volunteers had been mustered, with the intention of braving the frigid surf and saving the crew of the doomed schooner. Their purpose was a noble one. The reality was that no amount of man power would be able to row the little lifeboat against the prevailing winds and through that breaking surf—regardless of the intention. Time after time, the small craft was swamped, blown around and beaten back by Lake Michigan and her stormy allies, the vicious breakers. It became clear there was no chance of reaching the GRANADA. The lake had a death-grip on the boat's people . . . and would not give them up.

When she hit the bottom the GRANADA gave every indication that she would immediately go to pieces, her hull cracked like an egg and surf exploded over the ice-caked rail. So badly was her hull fractured that one of the crew fell into the crevice and was being chewed as if in the jaws of an icy sea monster as the hull flexed with the action of the seas. That was where Angus Linklater found the hapless sailor, attracted by his screams through the surf sprayed confusion.

"For God's sake, help me!" the luckless seaman cried to Linklater, as he neared the gap.

Risking his own life among the teeth of shattered timbers, Linklater went into the fracture and pulled the man free. He knew at once that there was no chance that the mangled crewman could swim for shore. Considering that the GRANADA was fast breaking up, it quickly became apparent that swimming was just what had to be done. In much the same way as he had cared for the expired cook, Linklater wrapped the groaning man in the canvas from a sail, this time in the hope of keeping him alive. Perhaps before the boat broke up the lifesavers might get aboard and carry the wounded sailor to safety in their surfboat. The gesture was compassionate, but useless. The GRANADA was rapidly going to pieces beneath Angus Linklater's feet and the local lifesavers were busy elsewhere.

Exactly how people think at moments such as this is hard to imagine, they stood on a wooden structure that groaned and twisted like a serpent as each towering whitecap smashed over it. What seemed to be an insurmountable distance of several hundred yards of breakers separated the shivering crewmen from salvation, but it was inevitable that they would soon be in the ice water surf, one way or another. Hastily, the survivors gathered a hodgepodge of wreckage, and what remained of the GRANADA's lumber cargo, and began to fashion makeshift rafts. First over the side was Owen Connelly and Michael Duffy—leaping into the churning waves with their raft clutched tightly, they were never again seen alive. Captain Linklater and his brother Angus followed, plunging into the sting of the bitter cold lake. Surfacing belatedly the

two men kicked with legs that they could no longer feel and gasped for breath after each wave slammed upon them. With his benumbed arms losing their grip, Captain Linklater was washed from the raft. Before he could be consumed by Lake Michigan, his brother reached out with the strength that only a brother can muster, and hauled him back aboard. In the process the timbers on which they were floating pinched together and smashed Angus' hand. Several waves later another powerful breaker slammed onto the brothers Linklater and when it was expended, Captain Robert Linklater was gone forever.

William Bissell went over the side and found the same frigid rampage that the Linklaters had. His raft was smaller, and crumbled to bits as he was washed off time and again. He was grappling for any piece of flotsam that might buoy him up for just another breath as he struggled, not to make the beach, but just to live for a moment more. Perhaps it was that will alone that kept him alive until his body struck the sand, or maybe it was the hand of Providence that cast him from the surf—no matter, Bissell was the first of the GRANADA's people to reach dry land alive. The crowd of locals quickly attended to the drenched castaway while a short distance away, Angus Linklater tumbled onto the beach with a breaking wave. As the surviving Linklater brother was helped to the bonfire, he saw Bissell look out toward the wreck as yet another wave exploded over it and cry, "For God's sake, boys, get a line to those poor fellows!"

By dawn Monday, the winds had faded to a calm and the snow had stopped. All around the Great Lakes, vessels had been attacked, but it was Lake Michigan where the most destruction had taken place. At five o'clock that morning, Captain Campbell brought the package steamer NORTHERN QUEEN into Milwaukee. It was the first boat to pass below Two Rivers Point since the storm had reached its peak. Captain Campbell reported seeing more than two dozen vessels, most of them sailing ships, flying distress signals. His observations, however, were only a pale sampling of what the storm had done. At North Bay, 23 wind-powered lakers were sheltered, 13 of which were damaged. The FLORETTA had dragged her hooks and been blown into the LAURA MC DONALD, which was carried toward the shallows and sunk by the winds and seas. Also ashore was the GUIDO PIFSTER, JENNIE BELL and L.M. ELLSWORTH, while the COLONEL ELLSWORTH and NAIDE had fetched up nearby with broken rudders. The

GEORGE MURRAY was picked up by the gale and slammed into the MONTAUK, badly damaging both boats. Canvas was stripped from the fore booms of the M. AVERY and BRUNOON, while the LUCY GRAHAM had her jib workings blown away. Around the lake, the reports read like a roll-call of lake sailing vessels. Ashore and wrecked at Whitefish Bay was the HUNGARIAN as was the CITY OF WOODSTOCK. The PERRY HANNAH, L.J. CONWAY, LOTTA MAY, LAWRENCE, EBENEZER, GAZETTE and CONTEST all were embroiled by the storm.

That Monday, the remains of those that would never sail again began to turn up. Some eight miles north of the Chicago light, the tops of the masts of a sailing boat were found jutting from the 50 foot depth of the lake. The schooner was later identified as the ore-laden DAVID A. WELLS, but none of her crew were found, and to this day no one knows what exactly happened to her. She was simply overcome by the storm. On the opposite side of the lake the flotsam of the ALPENA washed up and was intermixed with pieces of the TRADER. And what of the TRADER? The little steamer's wreckage seemed to be the final mystery of the "Alpena storm." Perhaps the mystery was caused by the fact that, despite what most sources may say, the TRADER was not lost in the "Alpena storm." She was sunk four days before the big storm hit.

To set the record straight, the steam-barge TRADER was guided from the harbor of Muskegon into Lake Michigan's choppy seas by Captain Frank Brown at seven o'clock on Monday evening, October the 12th. She had a cargo of lumber in the hold and some 50,000 board feet stacked on her deck. Bound for Chicago, the little vessel took just three hours to be overwhelmed by the lake. A massive leak developed below decks and she soon waterlogged and sank to her deck, with only the buoyant cargo in the lower hold to keep her from plunging below the surface. The seas surged over her until seven o'clock the following morning, when Captain Frank Fraga of the schooner GUIDE came upon her. With the seas rolling high, Captain Fraga maneuvered the schooner into a series of close passes to the floundering TRADER . With each pass, some of the steamer's crew would leap for their lives and tumble onto the GUIDE. When all were safely removed from the TRADER, the GUIDE left the scene and shuttled the 11 souls to a safe harbor. At noon, the steamer S.C. HALL stumbled across the floundering TRADER and towed the derelict to Grand Haven, Michigan.

Just how the water-logged Trader was swept up into the "Alpena storm" from the port of Grand Haven is quite unclear. The storm was from the southwest and would have been blowing into the harbor thus preventing anything from being carried out of port onto the open lake. What is most likely is that the HALL was unable to pull the TRADER, sunken extremely low in the water, into the Grand River and simply lodged her on a convenient sandbar outside the harbor, with hope that she could be pumped out and brought properly into port before the weather again came up. Apparently, before the little TRADER's owner, S.A. Brown of Pentwater, Michigan, could decide what to do with her the "Alpena storm" thundered down upon Lake Michigan and ripped her apart. The news of the TRADER's loss spread across the lakes as fast as the storm winds, and was woven into the horror of the big storm. Unfortunately, the correction of the facts appeared as a single paragraph in the Detroit Free Press and was easily overlooked—not only in 1880, but for more than a century thereafter.

To Captain Brown, the whole matter of the TRADER was probably an on-going source of aggravation for months to come. He found himself having to explain to his peers, each time that they met, how it was that he had not perished on Lake Michigan. Yet acquaintances that he had not seen in years greeted the good captain as if just returned from the great beyond. To the TRADER's owner, Mr. Brown, it was a loss of $5,500, roughly the cost of a good sized tug. Later he arranged for what was left of the vessel to be dragged to Pentwater where she is said to have been abandoned in 1883.

Through the use of a single sail, the MARY GROH managed to work her way more than 50 miles up to the port of Milwaukee, arriving with the loss of her deck load and one passenger. Later, with a full fuel bunker she proceeded to Chicago, and thereafter went on to sail an extended career before being scrapped in 1926. The GRANADA broke up where she landed, with William Bissell and Angus Linklater the only survivors. To this day, the schooner's bones may rest in the shifting sands two miles north of the Muskegon channel and just off shore. On the other hand, the sands of the eastern shore of Lake Michigan have a habit of descending down and making a beach where once there was water. Often, the people working on jetties, docks and break waters in modern times, have bulldozed the sands back, and found the skeleton of a wooden lakeboat once thought lost off shore, now buried well inland. Similarly, the waves of a contemporary storm will, on occasion, beat back the sands to uncover the ribs of a ghost ship.

It is a tempting possibility that the fair weather tourist, taking a leisurely walk along the beach at Muskegon State Park, may be walking atop the GRANADA's remains. Long forgotten are the frozen storm winds that left her on that spot and the desperate men who leaped into the frothing lake, clinging to bits of wreckage. If the readers of this tale should happen to stroll the beach of Muskegon State Park, they may do the GRANADA's people a service, by looking out a short distance across the lake, or digging at that innocuous piece of wood stuck in the sand—and recounting the story of the "Alpena storm" and the luckless schooner that rests near by. She marks the spot where the floating small business of the Linklater family came to its tragic end . . .

A Cold Water Affair

A typical mid-summer sun beat down on the wooden decking of the steamer WAVERLY, as she plowed up the Detroit River. Beyond the laker's port rail the booming metropolis that would one day become the "motor city" seemed to slip past in the summer haze—it was the 21st day of July, 1903. In command of the WAVERLY was Captain Henry Bennett of Bay City, and securely tethered to the steamer's towing bit was the schooner-barge W.S. CROSTHWAITE. There was nothing special about another steamer and her consort passing Detroit, for after all it was the middle of the shipping season, and it was not at all uncommon for more than 100 lakers to pass by in a 24 hour period. The WAVERLY and her consort simply blended into the din of river traffic as readily as the dense coal smoke from the steamer's funnel mixed with that of every other smokestack.

Both WAVERLY and her schooner-barge were running under the banner of the Alpena-based J.C. Gilchrist armada. Looking back across the years, an inventory of the Gilchrist line would read like a cross-section of all the boats working the lakes in this era. Giant steel-hulled oreboats were intermixed with wooden schooner-barges, and once-proud package freighters converted into the bulk trade worked alongside oak-hulled oreboats. The Gilchrist philosophy was to run their bottoms so as to gain maximum profit, at a minimum overhead. Often the boats ran without insurance, and at the first hint of costly repair were sold or abandoned. This method worked well in the

41

early years of the 1900s when there were always plenty of boats and sailors to be had.

The WAVERLY herself was a product of the rapidly-changing face of the Great Lakes maritime industry. On May 28th, 1874 she slid from the builder's ways of the Union Dry Dock Company at Buffalo, New York in a completely non-ceremonial launching. There was no smashing of bottles across her bow, or brass band, or even a picnic luncheon to mark the laker's first taste of fresh water. In the jargon of the era, this kind of passive launching was known as a "cold water" launching. When the local papers announced the WAVERLY's birth, it was accurately described as a cold water affair.

Constructed as a package freighter the WAVERLY was equipped with sideports for the wheeling aboard of barreled and bagged cargo, but the new steamer carried none of the topside passenger accommodations that others of the Union Dry Dock fleet were sporting. Like most boats produced at the Union Dry Dock yard, the WAVERLY had a hogging arch, but it was hidden below her deck, running lengthwise above and parallel to the keel. Her hull measured 191 feet two inches in length, 33 feet seven inches in beam and 13 feet four inches in depth, at 1104.2 gross tonnage. Deep in the stern a steam engine of the steeple compound type was installed. Cylinders of 22 and 44 inches in diameter were driven along a 36 inch stroke to turn her single propeller, so as to produce 450 horse power. The engine itself was the handiwork of Cleveland's Cuyahoga Engine Works and was considered to be state of the art in 1874. Just five days after her launch the WAVERLY was assigned the official number of 80432 and enrolled into service at Buffalo.

For just over a decade the WAVERLY served in the package trade, but by the late 1880s it had been decided to secure her sideports and press her into hauling bulk cargos. Iron ore from the upper lakes was under increasing demand and more and more steamers were needed to carry the profitable red fruit of the northern mines. By the turn of the century, the WAVERLY was toiling in the Gilchrist fleet by hauling ore downbound and returning with an equally profitable cargo of coal stuffed in her belly. Often the WAVERLY's burden was supplemented by a schooner-barge tied to her stern. Such was the arrangement on that sweltering July Tuesday in 1903.

As the two Gilchrist boats departed the Detroit River, crossed Lake St. Clair and headed up the St. Clair River, Captain Bennett's mind could not help but drift back to the ruckus that had occurred in this same area the previous summer. It was noon on a crowded Thursday, June 5th, 1902, and the WAVERLY was upbound with a cargo of coal, the schooner ANGUS SMITH in tow. Also upbound and passing the WAVERLY and consort, far to the starboard side, was the 278 foot steel oreboat LACKAWANNA. The powerful LACKAWANNA probably had a four to six mile per hour speed advantage over the barge-laden WAVERLY and could easily overtake the two wooden boats. This was the era long before the Sarnia Traffic Center was in existence to check and regulate the movement of lakeboats on the river, and captains were unquestioned directors of their vessels. So, what happened next would draw shock in modern times, but in 1903 it was not at all odd. As the LACKAWANNA started her pass, the master of the 251 foot wooden steamer MASSACHUSETTS, also upbound and in trail of the LACKAWANNA, decided that he was going to get the jump on all three of the boats ahead of him, and sprint up between the WAVERLY and LACKAWANNA. The result was simple physics and fluid dynamics.

A Swiss scientist by the name of Daniel Bernoulli discovered in the 1700s that as the velocity of a fluid increas-

Launched without fan-fare, the WAVERLY went about much of her career unnoticed. Today she rests on the bottom of Lake Huron in much the same manner.

es, its pressure decreases and one of the best ways to increase its velocity was to make it travel a greater distance, by placing an object in its flow, such as an airfoil, or a ship's hull. Apparently, the captain of the MASSA-CHUSETTS was uninformed as to the discoveries of Mr. Bernoulli, as he shoved his boat between the others. The velocity of the boats compounded by the opposite-direction swift current of the St. Clair River did the rest. As the water flowed past the hulls of the four upbound boats, its pressure lowered and started to pull all four together. As luck would have it, the MASSACHUSETTS pulled clear just as the LACKAWANNA sucked over and slammed squarely into the WAVERLY's schooner. Although the ANGUS SMITH was sorely wounded, she did not begin to sink immediately. There was enough time for the LACK-

AWANNA and MASSACHUSETTS to pull along-side and get lines aboard, in an effort to keep the schooner afloat. With all three boats moored together, they limped to Marine City for considerable patchwork and explanations. One year later in 1903, as the WAVERLY eased past the area of the past summer's altercation, Captain Bennett scratched at his chin, remembering that there had been worse days on the St. Clair River.

Just after dinner the WAVERLY and CROSTHWAITE passed from the St Clair River and crawled onto open Lake Huron. It was an amazingly clear evening and the lake was nearly flat calm. The WAVERLY's coal cargo was destined for the Youghiogheny and Ohio Coal Company's dock at Milwaukee, Wisconsin and in this fine weather the two boats should arrive at about noon on Friday. Both boats would have to snake their way above the Sixth Street viaduct along the South Menomonee Canal, and into the old Wagner slip to make the delivery, which would easily add a couple of hours to their schedule. Some 2000 tons of the black fossil fuel were heaped below the WAVERLY's oak deck, and the better part of a full day would be spent scooping it out once the boat was dockside. As Captain Bennett retired to his cabin he had few concerns . . . the boat was running like an old pocket watch, business was good and the weather was perfect for sailing.

At about the same time as the WAVERLY's master was drifting off into a well-deserved slumber, another captain was breathing a sigh of relief as his steamer cleared the St. Clair River and pushed upbound across Lake Huron's deep blue surface. From the pilothouse of the Canadian steamer TURRET COURT, Captain Black had made about the same evaluation of sailing conditions as had Captain Bennett. The barometer was holding rock steady and barely a breeze came through the open windows. Like his counter part several miles ahead, Captain Black would have a belated dinner and settle in for a good sleep. Running for the Canadian Lakes and Ocean Navigation Company of Toronto, the TURRET COURT was on her normal route between Montreal and Fort William, hauling the harvest of the rich Canadian grain fields. Tonight, she was running light and setting a brisk pace up the lake.

Unlike the WAVERLY, the TURRET COURT was a highly unique vessel, one of only seven "turret" boats to serve on the lakes. The turret concept was hatched in Great Britain, in response to the way tolls were charged along the Suez Canal. Fees for passage through the Suez were based on a vessel's "gross register tons," that is, 100 cubic feet of "space available" aboard a vessel being equal to one ton. Considering that this measurement was one of space available rather than weight, the wily British vessel barons soon concocted a way to cheat the tolls. On every bulk cargo vessel, there is always a little space in the uppermost wings of the cargo hold that remains unfilled, and when hauling dense cargos of iron ore, almost a third of the hold is left empty. What the creators of the turret boats did was to cave the boat hull and decking inward, to eliminate that empty space. The result was the hull had a neck and shoulders cross-section, and far less gross register tons to be charged with a toll. By the turn of the century, the turret boats had found their way to the Great Lakes, and were blended into the Canadian grain fleet. Aside from McDougall's whalebacks, the seven turret boats were the oddest-looking vessels to sail the lakes.

Darkness settled gently upon Lake Huron as the TURRET COURT churned north. Just below Harbor Beach the Canadian turret boat drew near the dim amber lamps of the WAVERLY and her consort. The mate had been watching the lights in the distance for some time, and knew well in advance that the TURRET COURT was gaining on the vessels ahead. Long before the vessels neared one another

the TURRET COURT was directed outward to pass well
clear of the schooner and steamer. From the turret boat
pilothouse the watchman could almost make out the elegant lines of the schooner-barge CROSTHWAITE in the
darkness. About three boat lengths ahead they came upon
the lights of the WAVERLY.

Passing of the slower wooden steamer was complete
and it was just a matter of time before the TURRET
COURT would be far enough ahead to haul back onto the
precise course for De Tour. About this time, the TURRET
COURT's wheelsman noticed his boat was falling off

course a bit, and attempted to correct. The boat failed to respond, and seemed to swing off course even faster. Frantically the wheelsman spun the steamer's steering control, but the wheel was useless. With a mind of her own, the TURRET COURT turned directly toward the WAVERLY and crashed into the oak steamer's beam like a hatchet into a hatbox.

On board the WAVERLY, the jolt of the collision had wakened most of the crew, either by tossing them from their bunks or knocking them to the deck. It took only moments for Captain Bennett to conclude that the WAVERLY was doomed. The TURRET COURT had been reversed in a tardy effort to avoid the collision, and now she was slowly pulling clear of the lacerated Gilchrist boat. As the steel bow of the turret boat pulled from the wound it had inflicted on the WAVERLY, the result was much like pulling the plug from a floating tub. The WAVERLY began to settle rapidly toward the muddy bottom of Lake Huron more than 100 feet below. Captain Bennett saw no chance for saving his boat and gave the order to take to the boats without hesitation. In minutes, all hands were rowing toward the CROSTHWAITE, with the WAVERLY groaning and gurgling behind in the darkness.

From the CROSTHWAITE's rail, the crews of both Gilchrist boats watched . . . and listened . . . as the WAVERLY simply sank. No spectacle, no explosions, no loss of life—just an old wooden lakeboat going to the bottom. The whole scene had taken around 30 minutes, with the TURRET COURT striking the WAVERLY at about four o'clock in the morning. From a historical stand point it can be said that the little steamer went out in much the same manner as she had started, in a cold water affair... of sorts. By dawn the CROSTHWAITE hoisted her sails and headed toward Port Huron with the WAVERLY's people. The TURRET COURT spent the rest of the pre-dawn hours

Showing all of the lines of a "Turret" class steamer, the TUR-RET COURT goes about her toil showing no guilt at all over her encounter with the WAVERLY.

drifting off of Harbor Beach, as her crew worked to repair the steering chain, snapped just as the turret boat was passing the luckless WAVERLY and the cause of the collision. After the steamer's steering equipment was fixed, she headed upbound once more with only a few scratches on her nose.

Odds are that the Gilchrist management was far less upset about the accident than was the Buffalo insurance company of Worthington and Sill. It was the habit of the Gilchrists to run their boats without cover of insurance, but in the case of the WAVERLY, they had $25,000 in coverage on her and $6,000 on her cargo—an interesting gamble, considering that she was their oldest steamer.

Today the WAVERLY rests on the bottom of Lake Huron nearly 150 feet below the keels of the modern steel giants that plod along the same upbound course that she once held. Her hulk is nearly buried in the muddy bottom, with decking and upper works torn away to the point where her engine works are exposed. Those who discovered her considered the WAVERLY so broken up that she was not worth the effort of a return visit. She's a cold water affair, at best . . .

When the Winds Moan and
the Snow Squalls

Oswego, New York was sleeping peacefully when the clocks struck the hour of three on the frozen morning of Thursday, November 24th, 1921. It was Thanksgiving, so the day to come would find most of the community's businesses closed down for the holiday. Calling 1088-W would ring the phones at T.F. McPeak's real estate and insurance office, but no agents would be there to sell those $500 lots. This also would be the case down at 136 East First Street, where Snyder's Electrical and Battery Service would display a "closed" sign through the day. There would be no ladies swooning at Rudolph Valentino's silent projected image at the Strand Theater, but "The Sheik"'s hypnotic painted eyes would be back on the big screen on Friday. All of these places would rest as quietly through the daylight hours of Thursday as they did now in the pre-dawn silence.

Down along the Oswego waterfront the scene was remarkably different. As usual for late season navigation on the Great Lakes, there was bustling activity. It was the traditional rush to work as many cargos as possible, before the coming ice locked the rivers and channels in its inflexible winter grip. At three a.m. that Thanksgiving morning, a small fleet of lakeboats was making its way out of the Oswego River. In their pre-holiday slumber, not one local resident would have an inkling as to the fleet's departure. Crammed into the cargo hold of each tiny wooden steamer was a pile of bulk phosphate bound for the Ontario shore. Puffing into the darkness, and marked by only a few dim amber lamps, were the worn wooden steamers HINCKLEY, PHALOW, JED and CITY OF NEW YORK.

Leading the ragtag convoy from the pilothouse of the HINCKLEY was Captain Augustus "Gus" Hinckley. The owner and operator of a number of small wooden lakers over the years, Captain Hinckley had niched out his own market in the eastern Lake Ontario and western St. Lawrence River region. Hinckley boats were contracted to haul almost anything that Captain Gus could arrange to drop into their holds. Coal, grain, pulpwood, and rip-rap stone were all carried commonly, and Captain Hinckley often had the contract for removing buoys from the U.S. waters about the eastern lake, before the Coast Guard took over that task in 1931. If someone needed something moved across Lake Ontario, a Hinckley boat could haul it. Furthermore, Captain Hinckley himself had a life-long knack for cheating the lake. An instinctive master mariner, he was known for sailing into the worst that the lake could offer and surviving.

Captain Hinckley's boats were largely those that had seen far better days and could be easily and inexpensively purchased from other operators. Once under the Hinckley flag, the tired boats would be worked harder than they had ever toiled before. The good captain had a habit of greatly under-bidding on hauling contracts, and then being compelled to overload his boats, in order to meet his agreements. Rare are the times when you will see a photo of a Hinckley boat without a heaping deck cargo. This is not to say that deck-loads were uncommon on wooden lakeboats, but the Hinckley boats were normally burdened until they were left with as little as a foot of freeboard. As a matter of routine, these old-horse lakers would be driven into all kinds of weather. Around the Oswego waterfront, Captain

Hinckley had become known as "the little old man with the leaky boats," a moniker that he did little to live down.

In the later half of the 1921 season, Captain Hinckley had negotiated another of his low-bid, over-burdened deals. This one was for hauling phosphate, most of which was bound for Trenton, Ontario, on the northern Lake Ontario shore. The problem was that there were not enough bottoms in the Hinckley fleet to come anywhere near filling the contract, so the under-bidding vesselman was forced to put out the word that he would be open to charters. The offer caught the ear of Captain Harry Randall, owner and master of the steamer CITY OF NEW YORK.

Captain Randall had purchased the CITY OF NEW YORK in the spring of 1921 as a replacement for the little steamer JOHN RANDALL, which had foundered beneath his feet the previous November.

Carrying 250 tons of coal from the D.L.&W. trestle, the RANDALL departed Oswego on November 16th, 1920 under Harry Randall's command. The burden of the 116 foot steamer was bound to R. Downey and Company of Belleville, Ontario as she beat her way onto a stormy Lake Ontario. About one half a mile off the Duck Island light, the RANDALL lost her fight with the elements and foundered, forcing Captain Randall and his crew of five to jump into the lake and swim for it. For most of the next week the six crewmen of the JOHN RANDALL were listed as missing on Lake Ontario, and nearly given up for lost. Fortunately, the lake had not been in a hungry mood that November, and was satisfied with the consumption of only the luckless steamboat. All the JOHN RANDALL's crew had managed to drag themselves onto Duck Island, and were found by Fred Bougard, the lighthouse tender. On the 28th, the weather had moderated to where the cast-aways could make their way to Picton, Ontario and tell their tale to relieved friends and relatives. All of this left Captain Randall in desperate need of another command. His search ended with the acquisition of the venerable CITY OF NEW YORK.

When Captain Randall took charge of the CITY OF NEW YORK she could be described, at best, as being in appalling condition. Constructed at Cleveland in 1863 by Stephens and Presley for the old Northern Transportation Company as a three decked combination carrier, she was originally one of many fine wooden propellers that criss-crossed the lakes, transporting passengers and package cargo. In her 18th season the boat was converted for use as a bulk carrier and thereafter began hop-scotching from one fleet to another. In the five years before Captain Randall acquired the CITY OF NEW YORK, she had been in the possession of nearly as many owners, finally ending up with the Toronto Sand and Gravel Company. She spent her first months under the Randall flag tied up at Kingston, Ontario where the good captain went in debt to the tune of $7,000, just to make her something near sea-worthy. By the time the word of Captain Hinckley's need for chartered bottoms reached Captain Randall, his own need to recoup his investment in the CITY OF NEW YORK's repairs was pressing heavily upon his wallet. With some haste, Captain Randall seized the opportunity and chartered up his boat with Captain Gus. Perhaps it was his hope to earn enough to fend off the creditors through the winter, and while frozen into the backwaters of Kingston, the boat could be brought into condition for a full season's work in the spring.

Holding his steamer in the wake of the HINCKLEY, Captain Randall guided her from the Oswego River and headed on a 340 degree course. His was a patch-work boat with a patch-work crew. In the interest of saving money, the captain had mixed his own family with the boat's regular crew, since the manpower of the CITY OF NEW YORK was just enough to make the boat go. Not counting the captain, there were only six able bodied sailors working it as deckhands, firemen, wheelsmen and all the jobs in between. Considering that the boat's run across Lake Ontario was only 48 miles, with an additional 38 miles spent zigzagging through the Bay of Quinte to Trenton, the whole trip should take only the better part of a day. There was no need for a big expensive crew like the long-haul boats. Mate Wesley Warren would double as wheelsman, the engine room would be worked by Robert Henry Dorey, and his brother Gilbert, who at age 17 was on the return leg of his first trip across the lake. Sharing the engine and deck duties were the Gallagher brothers, Joseph and Frank, as well as Warren Gilbert. There had been a fellow known only as "Sullivan," but just the week before, he had gotten his fill of either the CITY OF NEW YORK, Lake Ontario, or both and asked for his pay and gone "up the street." Another crewman, Charles Pullen, had done likewise while the boat was in Oswego the day before. Perhaps this was what spooked Sullivan, because Pullen had done the same thing a year before. That time, he had walked off Captain Randall's boat JOHN RANDALL just before she sailed off and foundered.

The remaining crew members toiled in the CITY OF NEW YORK's galley, and were all members of Captain Randall's family. Working as cook was the captain's wife who, in these days before day-care, had brought their 10 month old baby boy along. Lastly, there was 12 year old Stanley Pappa, the adopted son of the Randalls. He was put to work as galley boy, and spent most of his time swinging a mop, tossing garbage over the rail or up to his arm pits in dish water. Since these people were members of the captain's family there was no need to pay them, thus cutting expenses. Now all that Captain Randall need do would be to make as many trips as possible to attempt to break even for the season. Considering that at the rate of $2.05 a ton, the boat was earning $717.50 per trip—every crossing would matter.

No doubt Mrs. Randall and young Stanley were already rustling about in the galley as the family's steamer pounded her way onto the lake. This was where Stanley had finally found a place in life, there on Lake Ontario and in the CITY OF NEW YORK's cramped galley. Born in Scotland the lad was given to a workhouse as soon as he was able, and later was shipped across the Atlantic and dumped into a Kingston orphanage. At the age of eight, Stanley was discovered by Captain and Mrs. Randall at the orphanage, and the three of them made an instant family. From the first time the boy stepped upon a lakeboat, little Stanley was constantly pestering his adopted father to take him sailing, for presence of the boat and the mystical blue of the shimmering lake had totally captivated the youthful orphan. He was the kind of boy who would wait at the Kingston pier for the first sight of his father's boat, and bound aboard as soon as the gangway came down. When Captain Randall was away, or when his boat was at the lay-up wall, little Stanley would spend hours watching other lakeboats coming and going or just crawling on the distant lake's horizon. At last, in the spring of 1921, Captain Randall agreed to let his adopted son come out and work in the CITY OF NEW YORK's galley, whenever the boat had the opportunity to sail. Certainly, the boy went about his disagreeable chores with an enthusiasm that only a kid who's been waiting three years to get at it could muster. And it is a good bet that long before a hint of daylight that November morning, little Stanley was bustling about in his galley, like some pre-dawn naiad.

From the HINCKLEY's pilothouse, the view across Lake Ontario was ink-black, there were no stars, and only the

lamps of the other phosphate boats aft broke the darkness. The wind had been fresh from the southwest when Captain Hinckley led the leaky fleet from the Oswego River. At that time the weather appeared to be only seasonal for late November. But before long, Lake Ontario was giving ominous hints of what was to come. There was a "dead roll," or a strong but shallow swell that normally leads heavy weather. By the time the boats were half way to Main Duck Island, the wind came blowing out of the northwest and shortly thereafter the snow started. The seas began their assault on the over-burdened boats, and squalls of thick snow separated the rag-tag lakers from one another.

Shortly after sunrise, Captain Hinckley decided to tuck his boat up under the lee of Main Duck Island. This was a familiar shelter that the savvy master had used many times to hoodwink Lake Ontario out of pummeling his boat. At half past six, Chief Engineer Sweet squinted aft through the snow, over the HINCKLEY's rail. In the undulating distance the snow had thinned enough to show the silhouette of the CITY OF NEW YORK, about a quarter of a mile away. From the pilothouse Captain Hinckley spotted the steamer, which had hauled to the east and was now running before the seas. "Where in blazes is Harry headed?" the old master croaked, planting his hands on his hips. "Probably makin' for the Galloo," the mate speculated. "Well, he ain't gonna' get there that way," Captain Hinckley harrumphed. A moment later the HINCKLEY was pelted by the swirls of another snow squall, and the captain returned to tending his course. Down in the engine room, Chief Sweet was contending with a sizeable accumulation of water sloshing about in the deck grating. It appeared that a leak was developing in the cargo hold, but the chief had great faith that wily old Captain Hinckley would get the leaky boat to the shelter of Duck Island, in time to pump her out.

Seas were now boarding the HINCKLEY with fearsome regularity and creating a glaze of ice each time they washed aboard. The thick snow turned to slush as it accumulated on every part of the boat, freezing into rude piles. At about eight o'clock that morning the crashing waves seemed to subside for the rolling action of the HINCKLEY suddenly slowed. Captain Hinckley had found the shelter below Main Duck Island, and appeared to be on his way to outwitting Lake Ontario once again. The big lake seemed to become more enraged by the captain's savvy, for now the winds shrieked across the island and the snow came pelting. Warm in his pilothouse, old Captain Gus must have smirked a bit. He knew what Lake Ontario had in mind next—it would be a shift in wind, probably to the northeast.

Joining the HINCKLEY under the shelter of Main Duck Island came the PHALOW. There was no sign of the JED or the CITY OF NEW YORK, but with the thick snow they could be as near as a mile and not be seen. By now Chief Sweet had a foot of water in the HINCKLEY's fire-hold, and one of the crew reported four feet of water forward. The relative shelter that the boat was in would allow the pumps to work against the flooding, but it would take time to put the water out. This fact was shouted up the speaking-tube to Captain Hinckley, who responded that as soon as the wind shifted, they would pick up and move to the other side of the island. About mid-morning the winds swung to the north, then to the northeast, and the HINCKLEY and PHALOW shifted to tuck up on the southwest side.

By two o'clock that Thanksgiving afternoon, most of Oswego was preparing to sit down to a fine holiday dinner. The Hinckley boats had never had reputations as great feeders, so the crew of the HINCKLEY were not anticipating any such festive repast. Lob-Scow (a sailor's stew of whatever vegetables, meats and breads were around to be flung into a pot and boiled), of some sort would likely be the fare dished to the crew from Captain Hinckley's miserly galley. Most of the steamer's crew had been busy finishing the last pumping operations, as a majority of the lake-water that had come aboard was at last removed. Captain Gus figured he could make the dash of just over 15 miles to the lee of the Ontario coast, and still be floating. The winds were still blowing a pretty fair storm, but they were nothing near what had attacked the boat just a few hours before. With the PHALOW following close behind, the HINCKLEY churned from under Duck Island.

It was ten o'clock in the morning on Friday when the HINCKLEY at last steamed into Trenton, low by the head and obviously still suffering from flooding. Captain Hinckley had brought her as far as McDonald's Cove, and considering the snow and stiff winds, decided to hold up there for the night. Daylight Friday presented a far better circumstance for wallowing across the Bay of Quinte to Trenton. When the ice was chipped and steamed from the HINCKLEY's hatches and cargo, the clam-shell scoops went at unloading her. As the cargo was removed a large amount of leaking was revealed—eight seams had been worked open around her centerboard box and the water was gushing in freely. It was going to be a long day for Chief Sweet and the HINCKLEY's crew, but they went right to work pumping and patching. This was just part of the job when you worked for Captain Gus Hinckley.

Soon after the HINCKLEY tied up, the PHALOW came steaming in and shortly thereafter the JED. Only the CITY OF NEW YORK had yet to appear at the dock, a fact that was of little concern to those gathered around the wharf. Odds were that Captain Randall was either still squatting behind one of the eastern islands or, more likely, had run for his home port of Kingston after sheltering—instead of Trenton. He would at that point be able to run his cargo in along the coast, when the weather improved. But as the day wore on, concern mounted to the point where Captain Hinckley phoned Kingston, and got in touch with Captain Fred Baldwin of the Hinckley steamer ISABELLA H., there unloading a coal cargo. To his shock, Captain Gus was informed flatly that the CITY OF NEW YORK had not been seen at Kingston.

"They didn't come into Kingston," Captain Hinckley shouted over to the PHALOW, "Fred's leavin' there shortly and I told him to keep a sharp eye out." He did his best to mask his concern, for the CITY OF NEW YORK was an old boat and had been giving his friend Captain Randall a bad time since he acquired her. Captain Gus felt the odds were she had experienced a mechanical failure while sheltering from the storm, and was still behind one of the eastern islands. At worst, he worried that the boat had broken down while underway and was now either adrift or blown aground in Mexico Bay. Captain Hinckley could not but feel helpless. His own boat was in no condition to go out onto the lake and search, and it would doubtless be a day or two before he could put out onto the open lake. Shuffling around the HINCKLEY's little "phone-booth" pilot house, Captain Gus could but fret . . . as he paced in and out of the door.

Departing hastily from Kingston, Captain Baldwin decided to do more than just keep an eye out for the CITY OF NEW YORK—he decided to find her. Passing Simco Island he headed south past the mouth of the St. Lawrence River. If the CITY OF NEW YORK was adrift, she would have been carried down toward Stony Island and Henderson Bay. He circled Grenadier Island, rounded Point Peninsula and steamed into Chaumont Bay, finding nothing. With darkness setting in, he steered the ISABEL-LA H. into Henderson Bay and stopped for the night at Sackets Harbor. At five o'clock the following morning, the ISABELLA H. set out once more search, this time around Stony Island and Mexico Bay.

Just 10 miles southwest of Stony Island, the crew of the ISABELLA H. sighted a bright white object bobbing in the distance. As they drew closer, the object took shape—it was a battered lifeboat. Easing his boat's beam up to the drifting yawl would be no easy task, as the seas were continuing to roll high with slapping whitecaps. Gingerly, Captain Baldwin maneuvered the ISABELLA H. to the windward side of the lifeboat. With the steamer's hull acting as a combination wind-break and seawall, she got close enough for the crew to get a look at the horror they had stumbled upon.

Buoyed up only by the air tanks at each end, the yawl was badly holed, its bow stove in. A small sea anchor dragged along behind the boat, and the blocks and rigging from the davits were still attached to both ends. Frozen— one arm, shoulder and head draped over the side—was the body of a woman.

With pike poles in hand the crew pulled the yawl closer, and promptly wished they hadn't. Cowering beneath the bench-seats, in a futile attempt to avoid the slashing bitter wind, were four frozen men. For a moment all of the ISABELLA H.'s crew stood stunned. Then began the struggle to remove the corpses from the yawl. With considerable difficulty, the lifeless passengers at length were finally disembarked from their lonely dory—to forever. The yawl itself was hauled up on deck and turned over to empty out the water. The lifeboat and its people were all from the CITY OF NEW YORK.

Stowing the grim cargo as best they could, the ISABELLA H's crew again manned their lookouts as Captain Baldwin guided the steamer south, where the laker found herself pushing through an extended field of wreckage, nearly three miles long. At the far end of the flotsam they came upon a second lifeboat, similarly battered. The second yawl was devoid of passengers, and after that was determined the boat was cast adrift once more. Lake Ontario was showing its temper once again, and Captain Baldwin did not want to take the time to drag the boat over the rail. He made his best speed for Oswego to deliver his ill-fated passengers.

Oswego was abuzz with news of the CITY OF NEW YORK's fate soon after ISABELLA H's arrival at 11:10 a.m. Saturday morning. Shortly thereafter the grim task of identification of the bodies removed from the lake was started. The lady was easily identified as Mrs. Randall, and the others were Wesley Warren, Joseph Gallagher and the two Dorey brothers, Robert and Gilbert. Interestingly, one of the men was wearing a watch, stopped at 12 minutes before eight. The news was phoned to Kingston and Trenton, and all of the boats bound out of port that day were asked to watch for anything else that might remain of the CITY OF NEW YORK. Sadly, Captain Hinckley could but wait aboard his wounded steamer and monitor the reports of the lost vessel as they came by word of mouth. Not until Sunday was the grieving master able to put his boat back out on the lake, and running short on fuel, was forced to put back into Kingston until Monday. When he finally did start the search for his friend Captain Randall, Lake Ontario gave him only flotsam.

Lake Ontario decided to keep the CITY OF NEW YORK and those of her crew not found in the yawl boat. Most heart breaking of all was the loss of little Stanley Pappa and his infant kin. Some clue as to one of their ends may come from the position in which their mother's body was found. When all of the others were discovered huddled beneath the benches of the battered lifeboat, Mrs. Randall was found frozen, leaning far over the side with her arms outstretched. It is not hard to imagine her succumbing while reaching out in a desperate attempt to retrieve one of her children, plucked from her arms by the rampaging lake.

Exactly what happened to the CITY OF NEW YORK will only be known to Captain Randall and his crew. As of this writing, the boat's remains have not been found, so where she went down is a mystery as well. There are a number of tantalizing clues as to where and how the tired laker came to her fate.

First, there is the question of "where" Captain Randall's boat met the end. There are the two independent sightings from the HINCKLEY of the CITY OF NEW YORK hauling to the east at 6:30 a.m. and the fact that the HINCKLEY, which the doomed steamer was pacing, reached Main Duck Island some 90 minutes later. A simple time-speed-distance calculation from Oswego to Main Duck Island gives the two boats an approximate speed of just under six and one half miles per hour-consistent for loaded vessels of their class. Taking into consideration the dead crewman's stopped watch at 7:48, a radius of action can be arced from the 6:30 a.m. turn. Finally, there is the position where the occupied lifeboat was found. Discovered 10 miles southwest of Stony Island, the yawl was dragging a sea anchor, so had probably drifted little in the storm. All of this gives a triangular area from 16 miles due north of the Nine Mile Point cooling towers, to seven miles due south of the Galloo Island light and seven miles due west of the Stony Point light. The odds are good that somewhere in this area rests the CITY OF NEW YORK.

There are many assumptions in this location. Was the crewman's watch stopped when he found himself in the water? Was the time shown on the stopped hands a.m., or was it p.m.? And there is the matter of where the lifeboats were really found. The Oswego *Daily Palladium* states that Captain Baldwin came upon the yawls while searching " . . . the waters of Mexico and Chaumont bays, . . . about 10 miles Northwest of Stony Island. . ." The mentioned bays are to the southwest of the island, not the northwest, and the finding of the boats, as the paper stated, would not only be way out of Captain Baldwin's search area, but directly opposite the storm wind direction and far out of the CITY OF NEW YORK's likely radius of action. At this point it is important to remember that the newspapers of the day were hand typeset, letter by letter, by persons who probably had no navigational knowledge at all. The word "Northwest" is clearly a typo, the boats were found to the southwest of Stony Island, putting them well within the radius of action.

As to "what," happened to the luckless steamboat, there again are a few clues. The battered lifeboat with the blocks still attached is probably the best lead. It probably says that the CITY OF NEW YORK plunged to the bottom, with the lifeboats still at their stations. The force of the sinking would have ripped them free and beaten them substantially. With their air tanks unruptured, the yawls would have brought themselves to the surface. This same circumstance occurred with the famed sinking of the EDMUND FITZGERALD in 1975, but in the case of the CITY OF NEW YORK, some of her people were able to thrash to the surface and find the yawl. And there are the sinkings of other lakers of the CITY OF NEW YORK's breed. Hulls built for the passenger and package trade between 1856 and 1875 seemed to have a propensity for springing sudden leaks and sinking abruptly, leaving most of their upper workings behind. Examples are the EQUINOX and MENDOTA of 1875, ASIA in 1882 and possibly the MANISTEE and HOMER WARREN in 1883 and 1919 respectively. Too, there is Captain Randall's turn to the east, at a time when he was almost an equal distance from all available shelter. For some reason, he turned the CITY OF NEW YORK and ran before the seas and we will never know why. Perhaps the careworn steamer was taking water at the head and her master elected to put the waves at her heels to better protect her tender areas while pumping was being done.

On the last day of November, 1921 a small fleet of leaky wooden lakers sat wind-bound at the docks of

Oswego. This time coal-laden and weather-cautious, the steamers M. SICKEN, ISABELLA H. and HINCKLEY waited for the current blow to ease enough to make another over-loaded sprint through the jaws of Lake Ontario to the Canadian coast. In the HINCKLEY's pilothouse Captain Gus listened as the wind moaned through the coal trestle overhead. He could not help but wonder about the CITY OF NEW YORK and what happened out there in the snow squalls after he had last laid eyes on her. Like the ghost ship that she was, that image of the wallowing boat only 1,200 feet behind, belching black smoke and hauling east, was re-run in his mind, over and over again. If only he had known, he could have checked his speed, come about, tossed a line . . . something, anything. From that day on, every time the gales blew, the lake was churned and swept with snow squalls, that ghostly snow-shrouded recollec-tion of the CITY OF NEW YORK would surely stir in his mind. The least he could do was to remember his friend and consider the lost souls of the doomed steamer. When the winds moaned and the snows squalled, she came back . . . the ghost ship in the memory of the old man with the leaky boats.

Over the passing decades shipping from the port of Oswego has died to a trace, much like the story of the CITY OF NEW YORK and the lives that went with her. All that can be told of the vague disaster has been presented here for the reader to ponder, on nights when the storm winds moan and you just know that Lake Ontario is being whipped into a frenzy. Much like Captain Gus Hinckley, you may feel that pondering is the least that you can do for Captain and Mrs. Randall, Stanley Pappa, Wesley Warren, Warren Gilbert as well as the brothers Dorey and Gallagher—so that they, like the CITY OF NEW YORK, will not fade from memory. No lakeboat ever really "sailed away." They did on occasion founder with not a living witness left behind. Nothing is spirited away by some super-natural force. The wrecks simply lurk in the cold sackcloth depths waiting to be discovered. These are the true ghost ships, those that haunt the memories and imaginations of the people who learn their stories, see their pictures, remember their crews . . . and pass idle hours, contem-plating what happened to them . . .

Fire and Fog

*W*hen it comes to exploring shipwrecks of the Great Lakes, various persons have staked out portions of the fresh water seas and put down an informal claim, as both guide and keeper. The wreck strewn waters in the vicinity of Alpena, Michigan seem to be the turf of dive guides Bill and Ruthann Beck. Together, this husband and wife team work, to display and protect more than two dozen wrecked lakeboats, at over 14 sites on Thunder Bay and Lake Huron. From the giant steel salt water ship NORDMEER, which rests on the bottom with parts of her super-structure protruding above the surface, to the long-missing ISSAC M. SCOTT, capsized with her entire crew aboard in the great storm of 1913, the Thunder Bay Underwater Preserve is a cornucopia of spectacular shipwrecks.

Occasionally the Becks will run their dive charters out to the remains of a small and somewhat insignificant wooden steamer on the eastern perimeter of the preserve. As the visiting divers descend the 90 odd feet to the vessel they can move about her boiler, decking and open hatches. One fact, however, may escape the wet-suited tourists as they examine the wreck—insignificant as the hulk might be—she still carries fire insurance.

Business along the Saginaw and Bay City waterfronts had been slow in the first months of the 1894 navigation season. Obviously, the financial panic of the previous year was taking its toll on the maritime industry and the ripple effects had found their way to the shipping mecca that was the Saginaw River. By Saturday the sixth of June, the Third Street bridge that spanned the river between Bay City and West Bay City, was about 1,000 openings behind its 1893 pace, a considerable downturn by pre-1900 standards. The approach of the little lakeboat W.P. THEW at noon that Saturday would not help the bridge tender close the gap on last year's total openings, as she was to stop short of the span and then ease into the McLaughlin and Magill slip at the western foot of the bridge. Unfortunately, by the time the steamer was secure in the slip the stevedores had already put in their normal half Saturday of work and the THEW was going to have to wait until dawn on Monday to unload. Shortly after the lines were made fast, a substantial portion of the crew took the opportunity to go "up the street" to their favorite haunts or taverns.

Limestone, mined at Kelleys Island in western Lake Erie, was piled in the THEW's hold and would simply add another heap to the McLaughlin and Magill dock's numerous piles. Their facility was a clutter of assorted wooden shacks and structures, much like the rest of the neighborhood. There was a lime-kiln, coal sheds, work buildings and assorted unloading and loading gear common to the era. Adjacent to the McLaughlin and Magill facility was Moses Howe's River View Hotel, a small wood-framed structure with a few rooms that were rented by the day, week or month. Lodged beneath the hotel and extending onto the river was the boat house and small craft repair shop of the Lind brothers. Their business made its income from the river as well as the hotel, much like the refreshment stand of Albert Applebee. Connected directly to the hotel, Applebee's stand was the source of cold lemonade in the summer and hot coffee in the winter, and was frequented by the staff of McLaughlin and Magill, as well as guests of the River View. This small community was only a corner in the labyrinth of family businesses and industrial goliaths that fed off the Saginaw River and its maritime traffic in the 1890s.

Traditionally, Sunday has been widely considered as a day of rest, and this tradition was broadly followed in the 1890s. So, at three o'clock on Sunday afternoon the seventh day of June, 1894, most of those who worked along the Saginaw River were enjoying family hours away from their places of toil. Quiet Sundays were the just reward for five and one half days of hard work. But at Applebee's refreshment stand something was apparently cooking. Although Applebee himself was nowhere to be seen and the stand's doors were locked tightly, wisps of smoke curled from the vents, and shortly from the cracks surrounding the doors and windows. In moments, flames were licking the building's eaves and smoke began to invade the adjacent hotel. From his hotel residence, Joseph Crow detected the pungent odor of heavy smoke seeping in around him. Moments later he was dashing from the building, having saved nothing more than his life and the clothing on his back, as the entire building turned to flames.

Nearly every structure along the river front was structured of wood. It was cheap and abundant in the decades of the 1800s, But the wood used in construction was untreated and weathered to the point where it was kindling-dry. By the time alarm box number 2 was activated and the crew from the third ward hose house responded with their horse drawn fire wagon, Applebee's stand had been obliterated and the hotel was being consumed. When Chief Russell arrived on the scene, he saw at once that the McLaughlin and Magill property was going up in flames, and the entire west river front was threatened. A city-wide general alarm went out and the fight against the blaze began.

On board the THEW, only a skeleton crew were lounging about and odds are that she had no steam up. After all, it was not cold enough outside to heat the cabins and the engine would not be needed for at least another full day—so why bother to waste valuable coal by shoveling it to heat an unused boiler? The few crew aboard the little steamer were drawn to the rail by the clanging of fire wagon bells.

It was clear that something was really burning, and near by at that, as one after another the fire teams galloped up, and onlookers began to gather. Some smoke was making a haze and occasionally a pedestrian would dash by the THEW's slip. Shortly the smoke, spread by a stiff southeast wind, became frighteningly dense, and glowing embers began to rain down around the THEW. Almost simultaneously, the steamer's people came to the realization that it was the McLaughlin and Magill property being consumed and the wall of fire was headed directly toward them. There was no time to get up steam and back the THEW clear of the slip so, like many others near by, the steamer's crew simply gathered what possessions they could snatch and fled for their lives.

Along the full length of the Third Street bridge, throngs of spectators gathered to watch the blaze as the fire fighters did battle. Every fire rig from both sides of the river charged in to join the fracas and hoses were stretched into the river to syphon water. Armed with his assigned hose, fire fighter Frank Herrick was working at the perimeter of the inferno, applying liberal amounts of water to the flames. Moving the stream of river water across the burning scene, he inadvertently hit one of the electric wires supplying power to the adjacent streetcar line. With the speed of light, the electricity followed the water and found the brass nozzle that Herrick had a vice-like grip on. The aggressive fire fighter naturally got the full benefit of the jolt and awoke some minutes later flat on his back, several yards away from his thrashing hose. Bystanders scrambled around, trying to revive the stunned fireman and catch the rampaging hose.

At the base of the Third Street bridge the support timbers had become involved in the flames and Welche's lumber dock was being threatened, when the fireboat GEYSER hove onto the scene. In short order the fireboat doused the flames that threatened the bridge and lumber dock, and then the GEYSER positioned herself to go to the aid of the THEW—but it was too late. Although the GEYSER's powerful hoses smothered the fires around the slip, there was little left of the THEW. She, like most of the entire block, had been almost totally consumed by the blaze. All that remained of the little wooden steamer was her hull from about the water line down, and the cargo of limestone. Like Applebee's stand, Howe's hotel, Lind's boat house and McLaughlin and Magill's coal and lime works, the W.P. THEW had been flattened.

This was the second time in two years that the THEW had been burned to the waterline, the first being in May of 1892 when she incinerated her upper works at Chicago. Her owners, the Marine Bank of Cleveland, had invested some $2,000 in her rebuild, but this time it appeared the tab would exceed $5,000. Just why an insignificant steamer like the THEW would have that kind of money invested in yet another rebuild, during one of the worst economic depressions in U.S. history, is completely unknown. But shortly after the West Bay City fire, her owners decided to have her rebuilt once again.

In the THEW's favor was her age, her hull was constructed by Henry D. Root at Vermillion, Ohio and later towed to Lorain for the addition of engine works. Originally the THEW measured 132 feet in overall length, 23 feet in beam and a scant eight feet in depth. At Lorain, she was given a steeple compound engine with cylinders of 14 and 28 inches in diameter and a 20 inch stroke. This engine developed a minimal 400 horse power to drive her 106 net tons across the surface of the lakes. The little lakeboat was assigned an official number of 81024 and went straight to work, hauling lumber and bulk cargos. At the time of her second burning she could have been replaced easily by any number of vessels idled by the slow economic times but, inexplicably, was returned to service. For a decade and a half after her scorching at West Bay City the THEW hauled lumber, coal and stone around the lakes, scarcely noticed.

The THEW's cook was just picking up the dinner mess as the insignificant steamer cleared the Saginaw River and headed upbound across Saginaw Bay. The date was now was Monday, June 21st, 1909, a decade and a half after the Bay City fire had flattened her. Having delivered a cargo of 330 tons of limestone at the Boutell Brothers dock in Bay City, the THEW was once again going about her toil in her usual obscurity. Commanding over the boat's tiny pilothouse was Captain Duncan, and the vessel was running under the ownership of Hugh R. Harvey of Detroit. Another cargo of limestone was to be placed in the THEW's hold and hauled back to Bay City, so the little laker's steering pole was pointed toward Rogers City, Michigan on the northern tip of the state's mitten. Some 14 hours would be consumed in the upbound passage which would take her in an arcing course past Tawas, Sturgeon Point and at length rounding Thunder Bay Island off Alpena. Considering her history, it is not surprising to know that the THEW carried only one form of indemnity at this point in her career and that was, of course, fire insurance.

As the first hours of Tuesday began to pass, the few dim lights that had once flickered ashore faded from sight. The THEW's own lamps grew fuzzy, as the light they emitted became diffused by a thickening fog. The mate sent for Captain Duncan who made his way to the pilothouse, attempting to get his eyes fully open. Ordering the whistle blown three times a minute as a fog signal, the THEW's master rapidly calculated the time to Sturgeon Point. As per his estimate, the dim flashes of the Sturgeon Point light soon brightened the muddle; it was just before 3:45 Tuesday morning. Figuring to be off Thunder Bay Island at six o'clock sharp, Captain Duncan hoped that by then the dawn would have caused the fog to lift.

Standing atop the THEW's pilothouse on her open-air bridge, the steamer's navigation crew kept a sharp ear open for the whistles of oncoming vessels. To a man, they knew all too well that another boat could burst from the darkness at any moment and smash them to pieces. This was in an era when massive steel oreboats intermixed in the jumble of lake commerce with the fragile wooden boats. Too many cases had occurred wherein a giant steel boat had come charging out of the fog and plowed down one of their oak counter parts. This was an image that the THEW's people kept readily in their thoughts, as they stood their respective watches on foggy nights. The hours seemed to drag before the gray surrounding the THEW brightened. Everyone aboard the little lakeboat breathed a bit more easily as the mist began to loosen its hold. In less than an hour they would be off Thunder Bay Island and would make the turn toward Rogers City. Even if the fog kept up, the THEW should make the dock by noon.

Just before half past six, Captain Duncan was counting the minutes before making his turn. This maneuver would have to be performed on time, as the fog that once gave signs of breaking up with the coming of daylight, had in fact now grown cotton thick. The captain's concentration on his navigation problem was shattered by the shouts of the watchman at the starboard rail. An instant later, the monstrous bluff bow of a giant steel lakeboat loomed through the mist, on the THEW's starboard beam.

There was no time to swing the rudder, no time to kick in more engine revolutions, no time to blow a danger signal, no time to do anything—before the massive oreboat slammed into the wooden hull of the THEW. The tiny laker was lifted slightly by the impact and began to roll to port, and for a moment it must have felt like she was about to tumble over and roll beneath her enormous assailant. Before there could come another beat of the captain's heart, the THEW sheared around and pulled free of the steel steamer's bow. Bumping and rumbling along the oreboat's beam, the THEW was shoved aside as her attacker churned past. In shock, every eye on board the THEW watched, as the stern of the other boat was swallowed up by the fog, nearly as fast as she had appeared. The last thing distinguishable on the fading behemoth were the raised white letters on her stern. It read "WILLIAM LIVINGSTON."

Alone once more in a mist-shrouded silence, the stunned crew did not know what to make of the event. The shock mercifully thinned, and drew their attention toward saving their boat. The impact had sliced her just forward of the after cabin, and already Lake Huron was eagerly flooding in. Nothing that mortal man could do would keep the frigid lake from claiming the THEW—her hull was too badly damaged to provide any hope for salvation. Captain Duncan ordered the crew to the lifeboats, in the hope that they could get clear of the foundering steamer and pull for Thunder Bay Island. Abandoning the THEW went like clockwork and soon all of the crew were hovering a safe distance from the sinking boat. Together they watched, as the insignificant little steamer took her final bow from the theater of the Great Lakes . . . steeped in the noises that only a foundering wooden steamer can produce.

A protracted time elapsed as the 11 castaways of the lost steamer attempted to orient themselves. Figuring that

Having burned twice, the W.P. THEW carried only fire insurance when the end came. Unfortunately, she met her doom without a lick of flame.

he was about two miles off of the Thunder Bay Island light, Captain Duncan ordered the crew to pull due west. But no sooner had they taken their first strokes with the oars than the 450 foot steel steamer MARY C. ELPHICKE of the Federal Steamship Company appeared from the fog. The shouts and waving of the THEW's people attracted the steamer's watchman, and the big laker was soon easing up to the lifeboat. All 11 were taken aboard and transported to Alpena, where they were put ashore and shortly thereafter began to relay the adventure about town.

Just why the LIVINGSTON plowed down the THEW and kept going down the lake, is unknown. She had departed the Soo downbound at seven o'clock the previous evening, about the same time as the THEW departed the Saginaw River. She struck the THEW two and two tenths miles and 85 degrees off of the Thunder Bay Island light. This position puts her significantly off of the downbound track, so there is the possibility that Captain Craine, her master, was highly disoriented in the fog, but it is nearly impossible to smash a 545 foot steel steamer into a 132 foot wooden lakeboat and not have someone on the larger boat alerted to the fact. The watchman on the LIV-INGSTON would have at least heard the ruckus, so we can only conclude that those aboard the LIVINGSTON knew they had hit something. What is possible was that by the time the crew of the ore laden steamer got her stopped, the vessel's momentum had taken it quite a distance into the fog, and an already befuddled crew could not find their way back to the scene. This conclusion is strictly conjecture, as all that is recorded is that the LIVINGSTON rammed the THEW—and sailed off into the fog without a sign of remorse.

Forevermore, the little W.P. THEW will remain on the bottom of Lake Huron, a crumbling wreck half-buried in the mud and clay. Those who visit her may not think of her as anything unique, especially considering the other wrecks nearby. It is worth noting, however, that although she may not have had a spectacular or deadly end—and even if she was not a boat of any special significance while she was working—at least she had fire insurance . . .

Rudder at the
End of the Road

*G*oin' up north," is the term commonly used by residents of the Great Lakes region, in referring to an escape to the peaceful tree-lined bliss that exists beyond the industrial band, running from Chicago through Saginaw down to Detroit and along the south Erie shore to Buffalo. "Up north," sirens are few, fresh blue water is plentiful and the pace of living is slow and friendly. Nearly hidden at the ends of obscure two-lane blacktop roads are small towns, many containing small but fascinating museums. These secluded repositories of history are always worth the side-trip needed to discover them. One most worth the trip is probably the most difficult to get to, and it is the Great Lakes Shipwreck Museum at Whitefish Point. In fact, the venturing tourists may unfold their maps, scratch their heads and wonder "Just how do ya' get there anyhow?" Eventually, all who venture through the north woods toward the Great Lakes Shipwreck Museum will end up on Wire Road, which arcs along the shore of Whitefish Bay to the tip of Whitefish Point. At the end of the road are the gleaming white buildings and the tall spider-legged light that once were the light station and lifesaving facility, and now make up the museum.

There is so much to see at the Whitefish Point museum, that visitors may be overwhelmed by the models, displays and encased artifacts, and might just glance by one significant item. Standing like a weathered monolith behind the buildings is a massive wooden rudder. Running a hand over the oak planks the tourist may feel dwarfed by its sheer size and move on to the next display. Better it would be to step back and use their imagination to picture a wild lake, battered wooden oreboats, men leaping for their lives—and a boat that vanished in a storm. Those are the images that best suit what the massive oak rudder stands for. Running wild, the visitor's imagination may swirl back through a vortex of time to a long-lost past, and to a place not far from where the rudder at the end of the road now stands.

Foul would be the best way to describe the first day of October, 1901, on Lake Superior. With the bitter wind came a soaking drizzle bordering on sleet, and a sharp chop had formed on the gray lake. The steel deck of the CRESCENT CITY was glossed by the precipitation as she steamed across the open lake bound for the Soo. A pawn in the giant Pittsburgh Steamship Company, the 430 foot CRESCENT CITY had a belly full of iron ore, destined for the lower lakes. Astern, hissing steam escaped from assorted vents as the boat's engine throbbed below her submarine deck. Forward in his cabin Captain Frank Rice was just settling into his normal open lake routine. The hard days of Great Lakes navigation were beginning, and the CRESCENT CITY's master wanted to gain as many hours of blissful isolation as he could before the wearing part of the season pressed down.

Just over the horizon from the CRESCENT CITY, two quite different oreboats also were steaming toward the Soo. Ore from Superior, Wisconsin was piled in the hold of the 210 foot wooden steamer M.M. DRAKE, and the same was true of her consort, the 225 foot schooner-barge MICHIGAN. Although the three boats carried the same cargos, they were each a world apart. While the crew of the

CRESCENT CITY were treated to all of the modern conveniences that could be found in 1901, such as running water and showers, the crews of the wooden boats had no such opulence. As much as the steel-hulled CRESCENT CITY represented the lakeboat of the century to come, the wooden MICHIGAN and DRAKE represented the lakers of the century past. Unknown to the crews, Lake Superior had a plan to bring them together—under circumstances that none of the crews could ever imagine.

Constructed in 1882 at the Union Dry Dock Company yard opposite Chicago Street in Buffalo, New York, the DRAKE had the lines of many of the package freighters of the day. One modern source even lists her as having been launched as a package freighter, but other records do not show any conversion or tonnage alteration that would indicate any transformation to a bulk carrier. Without regard to such discrepancies, what is clear is that when she was launched on the second of September 1882, the steamer carried the name of the line superintendent of her building company, Mr. Marcus Motier Drake. Displacing 915 tons, the DRAKE's hull was flush-decked, meaning that there was no raised fo'c'sle and her pilothouse and forward quarters were simply planted at the bow. She measured 34 feet and five inches across her beam, and 14 and one half feet in depth. At her stern, an unusually tall thin stack became the boat's most distinguishing feature along with elegantly raked masts. As a package, the DRAKE was a floating symbol of her era.

Much like the DRAKE, the schooner-barge MICHIGAN was a page out of the 1800s. For many years the three-masted schooner hauled assorted cargos across the lakes, with nothing but the winds to propel her. Now the boat could only earn a profit tethered to the stern of a steamer. Launched on the 24th of August, 1874 the MICHIGAN was one of the largest of her kind, measuring 225 feet in length and displacing 1029 tons. By 1901 both the DRAKE and MICHIGAN had found employment among the red-hulled fleet of vessel baron James Corrigan.

There was no sunset on the first day of October, 1901. The darkness just settled in upon Lake Superior—as if Armageddon were to follow. With the darkness came the winds, spitting more rain and reducing the visibility to near-zero. From the northwest, the storm built waves set the vessels, on the courses to and from the ore ports, rolling in a manner that every mariner loathes. Aboard the DRAKE the rolling action caused by the seas was making a headache for two quite different people.

Aft in the DRAKE's cramped galley, cook Harry Brown was scurrying about like a juggler, trying to stow what loose dishes he could. Fortunately, the savvy 66 year old cook was wise to Lake Superior and her autumn temper, so most of his best galley tools had already been well secured, and now he found himself chasing a few cups, utensils and the odd saltshaker. Like every other galley czar on the lakes, Harry Brown was the repository and clearing agent for every bit of ship's gossip. Members of the crew liked to drop in for hot coffee to wake them or warm them, and at the same time catch the latest word about the next port or cargo. Also, the cook kept their bellies full with his hardy meals and their spirits high with his jovial manner. During the winter months cook Brown was the head of a family, with a wife and six offspring, but in the sailing season his family was the crew of the DRAKE.

At her bow, Captain J.W. Nicholson had been drawn from his cabin to the pilothouse by the rolling action of the boat. Tapping the barometer, he saw that it was already running uncomfortably low. The hum of the winds in the rigging, and the cork-screwing action of the DRAKE itself, said that all aboard would have a rude ride to the Soo.

Trailing in the steamer's wake, the schooner-barge MICHI-GAN had taken on a resigned roll. Standing at the open-air helm, the wheelsman had only his wet-weather garb to protect him, while in his cabin, Captain John McArthur Jr. was doing his best to pass the stormy hours with ship's paperwork.

Without regard to the downbound boats on Superior, the steel steamer NORTHERN WAVE was passing from Lake Huron, as the evening grew nasty. In the boat's pilot-house, M.S. Peterson, the NORTHERN WAVE's master, gave an unnoticed sigh, considering himself lucky to be getting off Huron before the weather deteriorated further. As the steamer passed Detour Captain Peterson pondered just how rough Superior was going to be.

The NORTHERN WAVE herself was from the same chapter in Great Lakes history as the DRAKE and MICHI-GAN. Built in 1889 at Cleveland's Globe Iron Works, she sported hull lines similar to a lakes schooner, but was 312 feet long with a 40 foot beam and constructed of prime steel. Her deck houses were arranged in the format of the package freighters of the day with the forward quarters stacked upon the spar deck just aft of the number one hatch, and the engine works aft. She had three elegant masts that were handy for dealing with package products, but her hold could accommodate grain cargos. Captain Peterson figured that it would be about two o'clock Wednesday morning before the NORTHERN WAVE would lock up. By the time she was on the open lake it would be near dawn. Only then would he know for certain just how aggravated Superior had become.

As the NORTHERN WAVE twisted her way up the Saint Marys River, the surrounding landmass disguised the force of the growing gale. By half past two o'clock in the morning, the steamer's crew were gathering up the lines used to pass her through the lock. Churning foam at her stern, the NORTHERN WAVE cleared the canal, heading into the inky blackness of the upper Saint Marys.

Perhaps it was many years of a schooner's thankless toil, one too many battles with seasonal ice or simply the direction of the seas that caused the seams in the MICHIGAN's planking to begin to open up. The winds were now howling at 55 miles per hour and the rain was coming in frigid sheets. On the schooner-barge's deck, Captain McArthur sized up the situation. The spitting raindrops hissed against his oilskins and the wind gusts were so strong that they attempted to snatch the breath from his lungs, as the boat's planks groaned beneath his feet. Foaming spray burst over the rails and mixed with the bitter rain. And all around, the lake roared. Despite the thick weather, Captain McArthur could see and feel the schooner-barge growing sluggish and a brief inspection of the hold confirmed the boat to be leaking mortally.

With all of their muscle, the MICHIGAN's crew took to the pumps. The process of pumping a schooner in 1901 could be described as hard labor, at best. Usually a four-man hand pump was used to expel unwanted water by elbow grease alone, but in rare instances some lucky schooner-barges had a donkey-boiler that could be used to power a steam pump. Regardless, a schooner-barge was equipped to deal only with small intrusions of water. When Captain McArthur saw that the lake was steadily rising in the MICHIGAN's cargo hold, he knew that her pumps were being overwhelmed.

It did not take long before the MICHIGAN's master concluded that his boat was doomed. His concern now was how long the schooner-barge had left. Considering that iron ore is a dense and heavy cargo, it would take little flooding to send the MICHIGAN to the bottom like a bucket full of rocks. With this in mind Captain McArthur set signals in an attempt to attract the DRAKE. In the stinging rain, numb hands worked at the steamer's windlass heaving in the thick towing hawser until the MICHIGAN had been drawn within hailing distance. An exchange of megaphone amplified shouts communicated the dilemma of Captain McArthur's crew. Odds are that the option of waiting until daylight to remove the schooner-barge's crew was weighed, but unhappily it was obvious the MICHIGAN was not going to see the dawn. The crew would have to be removed in the pitch-black of the night. In the prevailing seas, there was no chance at all of launching the schooner-barge's yawl—it would just be capsized or smashed to splinters against the MICHIGAN's hull.

To engineer the crew transfer, the MICHIGAN would be drawn up to the DRAKE, putting the schooner's bow quarter right up against the steamer's stern quarter on the leeward side. With the two oak hulls grinding together, the MICHIGAN's crewmembers were forced to leap for their lives. Attempting to time each crossing to go when the waves brought the two decks level to one another, the crewmen left the waterlogged schooner-barge one by one.

No sooner had the last of the MICHIGAN's people tumbled safely to the DRAKE's deck, than the wind seized the schooner and started to set her into the sea trough. As the MICHIGAN's stern dipped into the trough, the telephone-pole-like jib boom jutting forward from the forepeak swung across the DRAKE. With the wind square on her beam, the MICHIGAN was pushed the length of the DRAKE, raking her boom as she went. With a thunderous rumble, the DRAKE's after cabin was fractured, then her tall smoke stack was lopped off and shoved overboard by the boom. Those caught on deck scrambled to get out of the way of the MICHIGAN's protrusion, dragging forward, as if possessed. Forward, the DRAKE's wheelsman saw the carnage headed his way and managed to escape a moment before the jib demolished the pilothouse. Frozen in shock, the crews of the two boats watched as the MICHIGAN finished her rampage and was carried off by the winds . . . eventually to be swallowed by the gale.

Now the DRAKE and her people were in a deplorable fix. The loss of the steamer's funnel would prevent a proper draft from forming, not allowing her engine to get up a full head of steam. And the pummeled cabins and twisted door frames were utilized by the boarding seas, allowing cascades of Lake Superior to wash below decks. Badly-needed steam would have to be diverted to the pumps to purge the flooding. Without a full head of steam, Captain Nicholson could not keep the DRAKE from getting hung up in the sea trough—there was simply not enough energy coming from the boilers. Before the boat could blow around it was decided to break up the vessel's cabins to feed her fires. Wood burns hotter than coal, and hotter fires might provide the extra steam needed to keep the DRAKE out of the sea trough.

Having not an inkling of the M.M. DRAKE's plight, Captain Peterson was bringing the NORTHERN WAVE out of Whitefish Bay and turning directly into the teeth of the gale. The seemingly casual steaming of a 312 foot steamer into a 55 mile per hour gale, when in modern times, under the same conditions, vessels of more than double that size would be sheltered, is a true mark of the era.

Masters commanding vessels of the late 1800s and early 1900s simply sailed into what nature offered and considered storms to be part of the cost of doing business. Vessel managers and their ledgers would often ask questions about losses due to weather delays, that would mean the difference between a command and a mate's job in the next season. It is difficult to answer for such losses out of context, in the warm safety of the manager's office, so most of the vessel masters simply pressed on into the gales, come what may.

Stubbing her toe, the NORTHERN WAVE took spray over the bow as Lake Superior yawned ahead. All that indicated dawn on Wednesday was a brightening of the grayness that supported the whipping rain. Once above Whitefish Point, the seas began to come aboard the NORTHERN WAVE in a swirling ice water foam. It was a drenching that the little oreboat had experienced many times before, and the boat took to the lake like an old duck.

Shortly past six o'clock, the pilothouse watch spotted a strange sight through the rain. It looked like a barge, but was pouring smoke from its after quarters. It was the battered DRAKE. Binoculars revealed a distress signal hoisted upon one of the masts, and in a heartbeat the watchman was sent down for the NORTHERN WAVE's captain. Awake since the NORTHERN WAVE came off Lake Huron, Captain Peterson had fallen into a coma-like sleep as soon as head hit the pillow, in spite of the rough weather. Now, the insistent pounding at his cabin door had startled him back to consciousness. "Captain!. . ." the watchman blurted at the wooden cabin door, "There's a boat flyin' distress signals a couple of miles ahead!" The exhausted master grunted that he would be right up, fumbling for his slippers. All eyes in the pilothouse were now fixed on the wallowing DRAKE as the NORTHERN WAVE steamed to the rescue.

Sorry was the sight of the once proud DRAKE, as the NORTHERN WAVE came near. Crew members were going at her wooden cabins like a swarm of termites, with fire axes and bare hands. Pelted by the rain, a wheelsman stood among the ruins of the shattered pilothouse and every indication was that the DRAKE was in desperate condition. What Captain Peterson and the crew of the NORTHERN WAVE did not know was that the stress of the storm had opened the Corrigan boat's seams, and there was more than a foot of water sloshing the DRAKE's cargo.

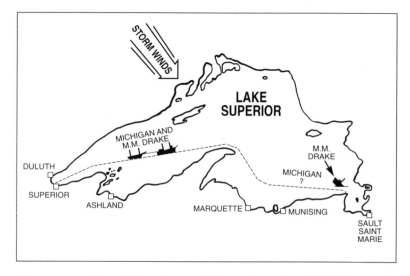

There was the distinct possibility that the DRAKE could plunge to the bottom with little or no warning.

Easing up on the windward side of the DRAKE, Captain Peterson brought the NORTHERN WAVE a bit too near the floundering DRAKE. With a sickening crunch, the seas slammed the battered wooden steamer into the steel hull of the NORTHERN WAVE. At that same moment, two crewmen, one from the DRAKE and one from the MICHIGAN, leaped aboard the NORTHERN WAVE. If they had planned to jump simply to escape or not, will never be known. What is certain is that every man on the scene knew too well that a bump like that from the NORTHERN WAVE's steel hull could instantly send a boat in the DRAKE's condition to the bottom. Pulling the NORTHERN WAVE clear of the wooden laker, Captain Peterson cursed himself for putting the two boats together—as if he could personally have controlled Superior's rage at that moment. There was no time for the captain to chastise himself, for he needed to plot his next move quickly, in the lake's enraged game.

Not wishing to bring the boats together again, he decided to put a line aboard the DRAKE and tow her to the shelter of Whitefish Bay. Closing on the wounded Corrigan vessel once more, the NORTHERN WAVE's crew gathered at her bow with a line ready to throw. Repeatedly, the thin heaving line was flung toward the pleading hands of the DRAKE's crew, and time after time the whipping wind foiled the effort. Happenstance rather than exertion was likely responsible for the line finally flopping across the DRAKE's rail. Numb hands pulled the lead line across the distance, and from the NORTHERN WAVE a six inch thick hemp towing hawser was fed out. The wave of an arm told Captain Peterson his boat was secured to the DRAKE, and he rang the NORTHERN WAVE's chadburn to "Ahead slow." Steadily, the hawser grew bar-tight—and immediately snapped. Peering aft through the rain beaded pilothouse window, Captain Peterson watched the whole effort evaporate in a wink. "Parted like a pipe stem," he murmured, beginning to pace around the wheelhouse once more.

The stress of the seas and winds were simply too much for towing the waterlogged DRAKE. Again the NORTHERN WAVE pulled clear, and through his megaphone Captain Peterson informed Captain Nicholson that he would stand by the DRAKE, in case the crew needed to be taken off— for whatever good that would do.

Everyone knew that the DRAKE was finished. The question was not if, but when, the Corrigan boat would take her death plunge. Yet even with the NORTHERN WAVE running nearby, the chances for those aboard the stricken steamer were growing ever more dim. The towering seas breaking over the DRAKE made launching of the lifeboats a near impossibility. Odds were that the crew would end up thrashing around in Lake Superior's glacial clench, from which few would escape. There was little comfort in having the NORTHERN WAVE standing by. She might as well have been on the moon.

Through the day, the DRAKE and NORTHERN WAVE helplessly slogged together. In late afternoon, the wooden steamer was dipping her rails with each agonizing roll, as her crew continued to pillage her cabins in a losing effort to keep up a meager steam pressure. As the morning had dragged into the afternoon, the DRAKE's inability to keep up steam had slowed her to a crawl, and the end appeared to be nearing. But, just as the situation began to look completely hopeless, from out of the gray distance a dark shadow of hope suddenly materialized. The steel hull of the CRESCENT CITY stumbled onto the scene.

Instantly, those aboard the CRESCENT CITY realized the desperate scene presented outside their pilothouse windows. There was the DRAKE, rolling drunkenly at the disposal of a furious Lake Superior, with the NORTHERN WAVE helplessly hovering nearby. It would be the CRESCENT CITY's massive steel hull that would be the tool to help rescue the Corrigan boat's crew. Being twice the DRAKE's length, nearly to the foot, the CRESCENT CITY eased up along-side the wooden steamer's beam, to providing an artificial lee from the storm winds. The big ore-boat's hull would block some of the rolling seas, to give the DRAKE's people a slim chance to save themselves. With both boats still rolling, there were moments when the two decks were nearly even—it was the time for those aboard the DRAKE to jump for their lives.

As the two boats slowly rolled near one another, lines were coiled in shivering hands, on both vessels, in preparation for the escape. At the DRAKE's rail, drenched crewmen rocked with the motion of the sinking boat, as the wind huffed past their stinging ears. Closer and closer came the plates of the CRESCENT CITY's hull, until it seemed each rivet could be counted. The two lakers rose and fell with the waves and seemed to be insanely out of sync. Soon, it appeared that the crews of each boat could reach out and grab one another. Perhaps it was this optical illusion of the CRESCENT CITY's true mass that fooled a frightened Harry Brown. As the two decks neared being even with each other, cook Brown got a leg up to the wet rail and leaped out toward the CRESCENT CITY. The big steamer was much too far away and Brown's effort fell pitifully short. The luckless cook plummeted into Superior's ice water abyss—and was swallowed forever.

Doubtless it was the sight of their good friend Harry Brown being taken to his doom that made the rest of the crew wait until the hulls of both boats were actually grinding together, before they made their jumps. Deep snaps, groans and cracking sounds rumbled from the DRAKE as her hull came up against the CRESCENT CITY. Each time that the decks of the two boats leveled with one another, more and more of the DRAKE's people bounded to safety. Just after five o'clock the last of both crews were thankfully safe aboard the CRESCENT CITY.

Exactly what the CRESCENT CITY's movements were after picking up the shipwrecked mariners is not recorded, but she ambled into the Soo lock at a quarter of two on Thursday morning, just over eight hours later. Down the rung ladder to the lock wall, the crews of the DRAKE and MICHIGAN klunked one by one, their feet glad to be on solid ground, their souls wondering when next they would be out on the open lake. Reaching dry land, captains Nicholson and McArthur collaborated on a wire to James Corrigan in Cleveland. The message would starkly inform him of the loss of his third and fourth vessels in just 17 months.

Most of the crews of the two lost lakers spent the day Thursday at the Soo. That evening, the whaleback steamer JOSEPH L. COLBY and her consort, barge 116, eased into

Sault Saint Marie. Both boats had weathered the storm moored to the ore dock at Ashland, forced to suspend loading and working the COLBY's engine, lest she be ripped from the dock by the gale's winds. At eight o'clock in the morning on Friday, the air at the locks was crisp and the sky was a rich autumn blue, as a number of Corrigan crewmen went up the ladder and boarded the Cleveland bound whaleback. The COLBY could not comfortably accommodate the entire complement of castaways, so some remained behind to wait for the next vessel headed Cleveland way.

The Soo Opera House was opening *"Don't Tell My Wife,"* on Friday evening. It was a part of the vaudeville craze that had recently become all the rage. If the next boat to Cleveland were long enough in coming, the boatless sailors who remained behind the COLBY could have joined the elite of Sault Saint Marie, for just 75 cents or the regular folk for a quarter, in seeing the show. Considering that the crewmen lost most of their possessions with the DRAKE and MICHIGAN, and that they had been wearing the same clothing for nearly three days, it is likely that going to the show was the last of their considerations. It mattered little, as this was 1901, and the next boat with Cleveland ore, the E.W. OGLEBAY was easing into the lock before Friday morning expired. Aboard went Captain Nicholson and the remainder of the MICHIGAN and DRAKE's people, bound once again down the lakes. All of them would be headed home, before signing aboard some other lakeboat. Only Harry Brown would never sign articles again.

On the Indian summer Sunday that followed the loss of the two Corrigan boats, Captain Andrew Campbell brought the steamer LIBERTY down to the Soo. Hundreds of locals garbed in their Sunday best were milling about the Government Park adjacent to the locks, and were treated to the most exciting news to hit the Soo in weeks.

Sporting her tall masts and stack, the M.M. DRAKE pushes downbound past Mission Point, a true classic of her era. Nearly a century after her passing, tourists of Michigan's Upper Peninsula can actually walk up and touch her rudder.

As the LIBERTY eased against the west pier, through his megaphone Captain Campbell announced to the crowd that he had found the sunken wreck of the DRAKE. He had discovered her on his way up Thursday and sighted the wreck again early Sunday, when the seas allowed for a close examination. The wreck was laying on her side in 40 feet of water with about five feet of water over her. According to him the hulk was resting between lifesaving stations nine and ten and he speculated that she was broken in half. All that marked the location was a floating spar, still strung to the hull. This was the last that was heard of the DRAKE and MICHIGAN. The bustle of events of the era again raised the cloud of industrial dust, quickly obliterating such stories.

Years turn into decades and decades build into a century and as the time passes, the losses of vessels that sailed the lakes turn into photos in a book, or a sentence and number on a shipwreck chart. Thus, the saga of the DRAKE and her people faded into obscurity. Decades of tremendously thick winter ice, mixed with spring and fall storms, smashed the DRAKE's remains to her keel, leaving only the boiler standing. The boat now rests upright on an even keel with her sides laying on the bottom, 40 feet beneath the waves. Her grave, six miles west of Whitefish Point, has become a popular site for sport scuba divers to visit. Curiously, the schooner-barge MICHIGAN has not been seen since that nasty October night in 1901, and there is no real effort underway to find her. She is too obscure to warrant the hunt. Most experts feel that she went down in shallow water, like the DRAKE, and was broken to pieces by winter ice-flows, and covered by shifting sands. But there is the remote chance that the ore-laden schooner-barge sank in deep water, and waits there to be discovered. As of this writing, she simply remains missing, an abandoned ghost dissolved into the rain-whipped blackness, on that frightful night in 1901.

In 1978 a group of research divers rediscovered the wreck of the DRAKE, and a year later raised her rudder, taking it to the Soo for storage and later display. These same divers became the seedling of the Great Lakes Shipwreck Historical Society, which later created the Great Lakes Shipwreck Museum at Whitefish Point. The DRAKE's rudder was taken to the museum in 1985 for display, in the yard behind the lightkeeper's quarters. Plans are, as of this writing, to move the rudder indoors to a future facility at the museum, to protect it from the elements. It is hoped the rudder at the end of the road will be visited there for decades to come. When the "up north" visitors view the towering oak curves, they should envision

94

giant, foaming ice-water waves, massive wooden ore-boats—and the image of a terrified 66 year old cook making a futile leap for his life—and a ghostly schooner, missing to this day. That is the real story that rests at the end of that long road out to Whitefish Point. It is only one of hundreds, waiting at that place . . .

Harbormaster Wagstaff's Vindication

*T*here have been times when the movement of the vessels that sail the Great Lakes has been so stirred by a moment, that even the names of those who captained and crewed them have been lost into obscurity. A case in point is the long-lost adventure of the 235 foot three-masted schooner MERRIMAC, in the tumultuous month of November 1883. There is no record of who mastered or crewed her at that time, their names have been long lost. The adventure of the boat herself, as well as the saga of several others caught in the same mayhem of nature, is worth telling. This at least allows that some names of other boats and people will be preserved.

As dawn broke on Saturday, November 10th, 1883 the Michigan skies over Sand Beach harbor brightened from the orange of sunrise to the rich blue normally seen only in summer. Gone were the menacing gray billows of clouds that had persisted with the storm of the past few days. Within the harbor, in modern times called Harbor Beach, an armada of wooden lakeboats got up steam and prepared to move with the dawn. Leaving the shelter they had sought the day before, went the steamers KITTI M. FORBES with two barges, B.W. JENNESS and four barges, MARY MILLS and her barge, NYLES without a tow, as well as the KATE MOFFAT and the tug RELIEF, with two barges headed for the Saginaw River. All had successfully ridden out yet another in a series of gales that had been sweeping all of the lakes since September.

Watching each of the oak fleet slapping into what remained of Lake Huron's chop, Harbormaster Wagstaff felt a certain sense of vindication. Recently, a number of marine columns in newspapers around the lakes had been openly printing the grumblings of unidentified vesselmen, charging neglect of the harbor by those who managed the port. One such rumor-bite ran in the Bay City Tribune on Sunday the 30th of September, quipping "A large number of reliable vessel captains complain that the entrance to the harbor of refuge at Sand Beach is too narrow, and that during storms it is almost impossible for tows to run in without being damaged. Complaints are also made against the manner in which the breakwaters were built being so arranged that vessels are liable to be wrecked by striking them. One old captain says that he believes more vessels have suffered there since the harbor was built than before." Such loose accusations had been causing the harbormaster unending grief, and his only consolation came in the sizes and numbers of boats that continued to seek shelter in his port. Pondering the tall-masted smoke-belching steamers and their tows as they slipped from the breakwater and headed onto the lake, Wagstaff bit his lower lip a trifle and crossed his arms over his vest. Apparently those "reliable," and "old" vessel captains did not mind his harbor so much when the storm winds howled.

Throughout that Saturday, the weather held its level of moderation and all around the lakes mariners, many set far behind schedule, seized the opportunity to get underway. Over on Lake Michigan, a pair of lakers were underway, hoping the weather would hold. Bound out of Chicago, the big two year old steamer ESCANABA was haulin' corn for Buffalo and attached to her stern was the schooner-turned-barge, MERRIMAC. Without any kind of weather forecasting apparatus, other than a barometer,

Sand Beach Harbor of Refuge—"One of the finest in the United States." Adapted from a drawing in The *Huron Times*, June 29, 1893

the masters of this hastily-assembled fleet had no way of knowing that yet another powerful gale was bearing down upon them.

Launched on the seventh day of March, 1882, the MERRIMAC was practically brand new. When she first met with fresh water, the schooner's hull measured 235 feet in length, 37 feet in beam and 18 feet to her keel and displaced 1398 gross tons. Hull 55, as she was designated, became the latest pride of the Detroit Dry Dock Company. She was enrolled into service on April 14th of that same year, with the official number of 91417, and went directly to work while the ice was still clearing from the connecting channels. Just under two years after her launch the MERRIMAC was making her living, towed by the ESCANABA.

Saturday November 10th, 1883 darkened into Sunday the 11th and through the quiet night, stars twinkled and the vessel lights shimmered on the subdued lakes. On Sunday morning a brilliant orange sunrise led to the echoes of coastal church-bells that could be heard well out onto the lake. Later in the day, as supper preparations were underway aboard the ESCANABA and MERRIMAC, the two boats were approaching the Straits of Mackinac and the sky had turned into a darkening haze. All of the lake mariners knew too well that the winds of autumn would soon return, and all around the freshwater seas expectant fingers tapped at barometers. Instead of an autumn wind, what swept across the lakes that Sunday evening could only be described as nature on the rampage. At Sand Beach, just as Harbormaster Wagstaff's clock chimed the four o'clock p.m., a green-gray wall of towering clouds, with rolling low scud clouds in the lead, marched straight across the port. The winds built quickly into a violent squall from due west, bearing driving, snow-spattered rains.

At the tip of Michigan's mitten, the ESCANABA was thankfully hauling the MERRIMAC out of the Straits of Mackinac, angling south to hug as closely as possible to the lee of shoreline. Still the winds and frigid precipitation hissed down upon them and the two wooden lakers began to roll in the seas. Building to gale force, the winds shifted to out of the northwest and howled, as Sunday wore on. Lakes Michigan, Huron and Erie were agitated simultaneously. Each of the freshwater seas was studded with tiny wooden freighters, schooners, and passenger boats—most of which were scattered like chips on a pond.

Fleeing the angry Lake Huron, vessel masters ran for the shelter of Sand Beach. Pounding in from the white-capped lake came the steamers CITY OF CLEVELAND, CHICAGO, PEARL, TOLEDO, ONTARIO, E.K. ROBERTS, WARD, TACOMA, OCONTO and QUEEN OF THE WEST. And the smaller steam-barges CITY OF CONCORD and her consort followed by the SALINA with a three barge tow. Among the fleet came the tugs JOHN OWEN, STRANGER, and PETER SMITH, the latter with a three barge tow. Three schooners came in during the storm, the CURLEW, S.P. AMES and MALVINA.

Heeling toward the breakwater beat the MALVINA, at about the same time that the tug JOHN OWEN was inbound, with the tug running to keep the schooner in sight. Unexpectedly, a burst of wind got into the MALVINA's foresail and split it like a sword. Without her foresail, the schooner quickly became unmanageable, an easy prey for Huron's talons. Fortunately, the crew of the OWEN saw the whole event and pounded a spray-filled path to the floundering schooner's aid. A line was soon made fast between the two and the tug pulled the wounded schooner into the safety of Wagstaff's refuge.

That same evening, the diminutive schooner S.P. AMES dropped her hooks outside of the Sand Beach entrance, having taken the same wind that attacked the MALVINA. Fearing that his boat might also have her canvas blown out, the AMES master elected to ride out the storm outside of the harbor. Unfortunately, the winds blew so strong that the schooner's anchors began to drag, and she became in danger of being pounded onto a boulder-studded shoal. Requesting the tug STRANGER and crew be put at the disposal of the lifesavers, Wagstaff sent the bunch out to the schooner's aid, and soon the tug returned, the schooner safely in tow.

Observing from the lifesaving station, Wagstaff saw to it that the storm-sheltered vessels were aligned in tiers of three behind the breakwater, with some aligned in doubles at anchor in the bay. It was the standard arrangement that the harbormaster had found presented the least obstruction to boats entering or departing. Without doubt, as the vilified harbormaster watched the numbers of boats at shelter in his refuge grow, he meditated how the opinions of vessel masters change when the storm winds blow and the waves crest.

All night Sunday and into the morning Monday, the winds howled from the northwest across the lower lakes.

Dawn on Monday illuminated the ESCANABA, angling from the Michigan shoreline above Oscoda in an effort to cross Saginaw Bay with the MERRIMAC. Her captain had chosen that point to come out from under the lee of land, figuring that it would afford the shortest distance to round the thumb, and again run in sheltered waters. Just before eight o'clock that morning, the two boats were in a quartering sea on their sterns and taking quite a dusting, when the winds started to blow the MERRIMAC around. Promptly, the ESCANABA's master ordered a maneuver to take up the slack and bring the schooner-barge back in line, but the stress on the towing hawser proved too much and the MERRIMAC snapped loose.

Undoubtedly, the ESCANABA's master considered going after his consort, but the seas were simply too big and the winds too strong to turn the steamer. And there was the cargo of corn to consider; this type of load rides like BB shot, and had already shifted, giving the ESCANABA a noticeable list.

Turning to go after the MERRIMAC was an absolute impossibility—all that those aboard the ESCANABA could do was watch, as the big schooner-barge was carried away.

Four hours after the MERRIMAC had broken her towline, the ESCANABA limped into Sand Beach. With her cargo well shifted, the steamer sported a severe list to the port side and was dipping her rails with each wave. The rigging was thick with ice, and white icicles hung from the entire boat like a thick fur coat. Little wonder as to why the steamer's master had chosen to duck into Sand Beach, rather than pressing on to Port Huron. Quickly, word of the MERRIMAC's plight spread through Wagstaff's refuge. Within a half hour of the ESCANABA's arrival, the harbormaster had dispatched the lifesavers to take their surfboat to the tug OWEN. With seas exploding over her, the tug slammed her way onto Lake Huron, in search of the missing schooner-barge.

Concern for the MERRIMAC and her crew was paramount in the port of Sand Beach. If her cargo, like that of the ESCANABA, had shifted, her people would be in a bad fix. Drifting with the seas, the listing hull would be boarded by every wave, and the spray from the breaking seas would quickly form ice in her rigging, masts and hull. That weight would threaten to capsize her with every whitecap that came to call. The fate of the schooner-barge and crew could depend on the tug OWEN, and nearly every person in the harbor town of Sand Beach knew it.

Hours of afternoon dragged toward dusk as the lake raged and still there was no word of the MERRIMAC. As the gray daylight gave way to the amber illumination of oil and gas lamps, frail lights rolled in from the heaving lake. It was the tug OWEN returning with her decks well iced, but nothing in tow except the lifesaver's surfboat. As the drenched tug eased up toward the lifesaving station, the station crew hopped ashore. They had searched as best they could, but could make scant progress in the towering seas. They had probably covered only a few miles in the six or so hours that they had been out. Considering that the tug's normal speed was about a dozen miles per hour, there was about enough time to approximate an intercept course to the MERRIMAC's probable drift, and sail out— hoping to stumble across the helpless schooner-barge. Once on the scene, there was just enough time to look around and zigzag a bit before attempting to beat the sunset back to port. With her windows covered with frozen spray and the spume and sleet cutting the visibility to near zero, the tug might have sailed right past the floundering MERRIMAC.

Into the night the gale continued its roar, and in the wee hours of Tuesday morning shifted its winds around to the southwest. As the morning did its lazy impression of dawn, the crew of the ESCANABA were still busy at the chore of re-trimming her shifted cargo. A telegraph report from Goderich, Ontario reported an unidentified three-masted schooner had blown ashore and was flying her flag at half-mast. It was immediately reckoned that this was the MERRIMAC and the tug OWEN set out once more, at half past one o'clock that afternoon, to try to recover the missing schooner-barge. Heading east-southeast as she cleared the harbor, the tug was swallowed by the storm.

Shortly after she set out, the tug OWEN was beaten back by Lake Huron. Nowhere near the Canadian coast, her master decided that the storm was still more than he had a mind to be in. Also sliding through the breakwater at Wagstaff's port came the schooners D. VANCE, C.G. TRUMPFF and MELVIN S. BACON, all feeling relieved and lucky to be off of Lake Huron. The masters of two of the vessels already in port were apparently unimpressed by the number of boats that continued to arrive, seeking shelter. Getting up steam, the tug PETER SMITH and steam-barge SALINA, each with a three-barge tow, cast off their lines and headed out onto the lake. Past the astonished eyes of a score of vesselmen, the fleet of six paraded, as if the storm were of little consequence. Before midnight, all six came slinking back into Sand Beach, their wires thick with ice. Saginaw Bay was uncrossable . . . the southwest gale sent punishing seas marching its full length.

In the frigid blackness of that wild Tuesday night, the 250 foot wooden package freighter WISSAHICKON came in—looking like an ice-sculpture. Immediately her master put the word out that the WISSAHICKON had lost her schooner-barge consort SCHUYKILL. Like the ESCANABA, the WISSAHICKON had been hauling across Saginaw Bay when the storm exacted its toll with the towing apparatus. Apparently, when the WISSAHICKON came about to head for Port Huron the towing hawser parted—and there was another schooner-barge adrift on Lake Huron.

Unlike the MERRIMAC, the SCHUYKILL's plight ended quickly. Late into the night, the lifesavers spotted a vessel at anchor just outside the harbor entrance, signaling for assistance with a torch. Manning their surfboat, the weary lifesavers made the drenched bitter-cold pull out to the stricken laker, and found that it was the SCHUYKILL. She had made it to the port on just her storm sails, but was not maneuverable enough to get inside the breakwater. The torch was signaling for a tug, and armed with that information the lifesavers rowed back into the harbor, and sent the tug OWEN out. Before long the SCHUYKILL was pulled off the lake and reunited with her steamer.

Frazzled to the point of exhaustion, was how the Sand Beach lifesavers started Wednesday morning. They had been at work aboard the tug OWEN nearly the entire night, and soggy articles of clothing were draped about the pot-bellied stove and brick fireplace of the lifesaving station. There had been just enough time for a brief breather and some hot coffee, before the lifesavers were again called to duty. Word came to the station that daylight had revealed a three-masted schooner at anchor a mile outside of the piers, through the night. The schooner was displaying a flag, indicating she wanted assistance into the harbor. Once more, the lifesavers and the tug OWEN struggled through the breakwater, perhaps nursing a hope that the three-master might be the MERRIMAC. They found, instead, the 196 foot EDWARD KELLEY. Pulling up smartly to the beleaguered schooner, the OWEN's men heaved a line aboard and moored the wind-grabber to the tug's stern and the distressed but thankful laker soon was safely tucked away in Wagstaff's refuge.

As uncertainty over the fate of the MERRIMAC grew around the harbor, mauled vessels continued to gather in escape of the maelstrom. The big wooden package freighter B.W. BLANCHARD came in Wednesday followed by the 1203 ton steamer ARABIA. Later the cutter FESSENDEN and schooner SEA BIRD sought shelter along with the tug MARTIN, which had been on its way to Southampton to aid the steamers MANITOBA and QUEBEC, blown ashore there. Both boats had been freed, eliminating the need for the tug, so the MARTIN waited to be re-dispatched.

But, what of the MERRIMAC? Reports from Goderich stated that the schooner ashore there was not the ESCANABA's missing consort, but a Milwaukee based schooner. As Wednesday drew to a close there was still no word of the missing schooner-barge, and the gale winds persisted at Sand Beach harbor. As Harbormaster Wagstaff looked out across his safe haven, he could not help but feel that at least one boat's spars were missing from the forest of masts over which he governed. What indeed had become of the MERRIMAC?

As the four day storm's winds continued on Thursday morning the missing schooner-barge was about to be given up for lost. Early that same morning at Sand Beach, the harbor town's telegraph at last clicked with the coded word that the MERRIMAC was ashore at Kincardine, Ontario, 30 miles north of Goderich. And for the third time in four days, the tug OWEN beat her way out onto Lake Huron in quest of the schooner. This time the MERRIMAC's location was known to the tug's crew. Or so they thought.

When the OWEN rolled toward the Canadian shore, all eyes were fixed on the tilting horizon. The tug steamed up and down the coast off the village of Kincardine, but there was no sign of the MERRIMAC, or any other vessel. There was only the beach and the breaking surf to mock the puzzled crew of the tug. Perhaps the hapless MERRIMAC had become one of those ghost ships, reported to be here

. . . or there. . . but vanishing by the time help arrived. Or maybe she had been blown ashore only to be smashed to splinters by the surf beneath the feet of her terrified crew before the OWEN could get to her. No doubt as those aboard the tug scanned the churning distance, they half expected to see wreckage and bodies on the waves or the beach.

Unknown to the OWEN's people, a second tug, the TORRENT had already removed the MERRIMAC, and was just over the horizon hauling for Port Huron with her prize. She had beaten the OWEN to a hefty recovery fee by only a few hours. Having found no trace of the MERRIMAC, the tug OWEN sulked back to Sand Beach, with the distinct impression that the schooner-barge had gone the way of the ghost ships. Hours later, the TORRENT and MERRIMAC entered the St. Clair River, with the beaten schooner-barge listing severely and near to sinking. Her cargo hold was flooded, cargo shifted and sails blasted into rags, but the people were safe. She was not a ghost ship at all.

For several more days the gales repeatedly swept the lakes. With the persistent storm winds, more boats gathered in Sand Beach's harbor of refuge—until the whole port was a sea of masts intermingled with a haze of coal smoke. Lakers of every description were sheltered in Harbormaster Wagstaff's sanctuary. Nearly a week after the blow had started, the winds at long last began to moderate and the snows turned to flurries. One by one the sheltered vessels departed Sand Beach harbor and with each passage, Wagstaff and his port were vindicated. The words of criticism, so haphazardly printed in marine columns, rang hollow in the harbormaster's memory, with the sounding of each thankful steam whistle that signaled each boat's departure. "Impossible for tows to run in without being damaged. . . I jolly buck want to hear that large number of reliable vessel captains' complain now" the harbor master may well have grunted to the lifesavers.

*The one-time schooner-barge MERRIMAC was later convert-
ed into a steamer and went on to work for many years
under her own power. Until now, few people knew what the
old boat meant to Harbormaster Wagstaff.*

The wayward barge MERRIMAC remained a schooner
for only a short time, after her tangle with Lake Huron.
Over the winter of 1883 she was returned to the Detroit
Dry Dock Company for conversion to a steam propeller.
Although there is no record of why this decision was
made, the odds are that her beating on the Canadian coast
the previous November inflicted enough repair cost to warrant the conversion. On April 23, 1884, just five months
after she had been mauled by Lake Huron, the MERRI-
MAC steamed from the Detroit Dry Dock Company under
her own power, sporting a fore and aft compound steam
engine with a modest 485 horse power. The whole contrap-
tion was fired by a fire-box boiler measuring nine by 16
feet, and constructed especially for her at the Buhl Iron
Works of Detroit.

For another 40 seasons the MERRIMAC sailed the
lakes as a steamer, being renamed ROCK FERRY and sold

Canadian in 1911. By 1924, however, the boat's worn timbers were showing their age and she was simply abandoned and left to rot at Ogdensburg, New York. It was a sad end to a hard working lakeboat, but interestingly, she had outlived her former consort, ESCANABA, by nearly a quarter of a century. The ESCANABA was renamed BALTIMORE in 1899 and foundered in Lake Huron off of Au Sable Point in May of 1901. She was running for shelter from a spring storm when a huge wave lifted her high and slammed her bow-first into the sandy bottom. The impact shattered her hull just aft of her forward deck house, and second wave swept the broken boat, demolishing her upper works. Only two members of the crew survived. (The whole story of the BALTIMORE can be read in this author's first book, "Stormy Seas.")

Today Wagstaff's refuge port has a new name, Harbor Beach, which the city fathers felt would better imply its true nature as a place of shelter for lake vessels. But over the years, the lakeboats have physically outgrown the port, and rare are the times when any of them put in to wait for weather. On the southern shore of the harbor, hidden among the discarded machinery of the local sweetening products plant, rests the original lifesaving station, (the first of three). Only a sagging roof over collapsed wooden walls remains today. The chimney—that vented the fireplace where dried the soaked clothing of the gallant lifesavers—is nothing more than a pile of scattered bricks. Walking about these ruins, with the whistling Lake Huron winds working at the rotting planks and the squealing of the gulls intermixed, one can almost hear the shouts of the surfmen and see the image of an authoritative Harbormaster Wagstaff. . . sporting his bowler hat, heavy woolen overcoat and feeling quite vindicated . . . on that exact spot, more than a century ago.

Signature of Misfortune

*F*rom off Lake Superior the bitter storm winds still came howling. Boatswain John Janssens stood at his post atop the lookout tower of the Vermillion Point Coast Guard station. There was no rain or snow, only the pure bitter wind lashing at him. It was the fifth day of November, 1925 and in the distance Janssens had in view a number of dim amber lights on the heaving lake. For a long time the Coast Guardsman watched the flickering lamps, for they appeared to not move at all. He speculated that he was watching a steamer and her barge headed for the shelter of Whitefish Bay, although observing their progress was much akin to watching a clock run. It was difficult to tell if the boats were actually moving, or perhaps anchored or maybe even in distress. The crew at the Crisp Point station would have a better perspective of the situation, as the lights seemed directly off of their location.

A half dozen miles to the west, at the Crisp Point station, Captain Joe Singleton, his son Tom, and two other keepers had been playing cards, when the phone rang. From the Vermillion Point station they were calling to ask about the vessel lights. The Crisp Point crew easily had them in sight, as the lights appeared to be less than a mile off shore. Responding that they would keep an eye on the vessels, the Crisp Point crew tried to put Janssens' concerns to rest, but the Vermillion Point boatswain would not be put off, and made a number of additional calls, asking about the two vessels. At length, the Crisp Point keepers convinced Janssens that they were indeed keeping close track of the vessels, which were showing no signals of distress.

Janssens held out hope that no grief should come to the boats, since he would certainly be one who would have to go to the rescue, and tonight was not the night that he wanted to be out on Superior. There was the consideration of the crews out there and how badly they probably wanted to be snugly tucked behind Whitefish Point, sheltered from the wind and waves. Feeling that the Crisp Point crew had the matter under watch, the Vermillion station's boatswain reluctantly decided it was time to tend to other matters of his own station. "Well, looks like they're gonna' make the point" he reassured himself, as he checked the clock and turned to his log. It was 9:36 p.m., and when Janssens glanced back toward the lake—the lights were still visible.

At about the time the watch at Vermillion Point gave up on the lights, Joe Singleton decided that he wanted a better idea of how much the boats were moving. With that in mind, he sent his son Tom out to place two sticks out in the front of the station, so they would have some frame of reference to judge the vessel's progress. Dutifully, young Tom found his sticks and marched off toward the beach. Lake Superior's crashing surf and screaming wind drowned out every sound, and the bitter cold stung the skin. Planting the sticks so the station light would illuminate them, Tom looked up to check the vessel lights again. It was clear that the seas were tremendous—the lights were rising high then dropping down and disappearing into the blackness as they dipped between the waves. But that was the only motion. The vessels appeared to be making no headway at all. As the lights disappeared behind one particular wave, those of the barge did not reappear and the illumination of the steamer at the stern went out.

The steamer then appeared to make progress and sailed off to the east.

Shrill rings of the telephone interrupted Boatswain Janssens' early morning routine the following day. On the line was the station at Whitefish Point, with the news that wreckage from a wooden vessel was reported washing up on the west side of the point. With that news, Janssens quickly went to work helping muster a sizable beach patrol in an effort to scour the shoreline near the station. The winds were still blowing at gale force and the lake was beating against the sands with the roar of unceasing thunder, which made it difficult to talk without shouting. Superior had turned as close to an angry gray as the normally brilliant blue lake can get . . . but only the surf lent a clue to what she had done.

Throughout the day Friday, the surfmen found the signature of misfortune sculpted into the beach by Lake Superior. Countless pieces of pulpwood were spit from the surf and lay partially buried in the sand—from six miles east of the Vermillion station to three and one half miles west of Whitefish Point. There seemed to be far too much of it than anyone would expect to come from a single boat. Amongst the pulpwood was found a couple of pike poles, an icebox and a piece of wreckage with a man's garter snagged on a protruding nail. The shattered stern section of a yawl boat tumbled in with the surf. Examining it closely, the searchers determined it to be the section immediately surrounding the socket where a sculling oar would be fixed, but no vessel name could be seen. Finally, one of the surfmen stumbled across what everyone had been looking for, but hoped not to find. It was a ship's nameboard—with the moniker J.L. CRANE painted in recessed black letters.

Two days prior to the wreckage being found on the beach, the wooden lumber hooker HERMAN H. HETTLER had just topped off a full load of pulpwood. She had spent the better part of two days at the Pigeon River, which makes up part of the boarder between the United States and Canada on the north shore of Lake Superior, taking on her pulpwood burden. With the HETTLER, and taking a respectable cargo of pulpwood, was the schooner-barge J.L. CRANE. Both were in the employ of O.W. Blodgett of Bay City, Michigan and were among the last of a dwindling breed of lumber carriers working the Great Lakes. By 1925, most of the U.S. lumber camps, as well as most of the saw mills around the lakes, had been long extinct. The wide use of masonry in construction, along with the concentration of logging in the Pacific Northwest, had diminished the lakes lumbering industry to a shadow of what it was three decades earlier. The lumber boats had been reduced to hauling pulpwood and rough-cut lumber from obscure Canadian ports to the few remaining mills on the lower lakes. Unknown to anyone on the lakes, the stock market crash and the great depression lay just four years away, and would spell the termination of lumber on the lakes, and the end of the wooden lakeboat. This was the end of an era.

O.W. Blodgett ran the last of the big lumber fleets, with a number of small steamers and several cut-down schooners, acting as barges. His was a no frills business, and comfort and accommodations took a distant back seat to operating costs. This was a fact that led to the crews of the Blodgett boats originating from the lower portions of the vesselman's hiring pool. This is not to say that the officers and licensed crew were in any way careless. The facts were that able-bodied seamen and engine crews who could ship out on the big, comfortable, modern vessels would have readily done so. These were boom times in the other realms of lake shipping, and even the big carriers sometimes had to scrape the bottom to properly staff their boats. The antiquated fleets, such as Blodgett's, were left with whoever they could get to fill whatever openings came up. For the most part, the unlicensed crews of these damp, smelly old wooden boats were drifters, and port-town nomads, often prone to the over consumption of demon rum. Often these individuals would come aboard long enough to earn the income of a trip or two, and then disappear back into the muddle that hangs around the taverns, speakeasies and drunk-tanks so much a part of that lifestyle. These were also the days of prohibition in the U.S., which made the situation on the lumber boats, which often tied up at liquor-legal Canadian ports, even worse.

As a direct result of these drifting seamen, the names of but three of the schooner-barge J.L. CRANE's crew of seven, were recorded. Master of the CRANE was Captain Richard B. Briggs, a Detroit native who found himself among the last of the schooner-barge skippers. The mate was John Bonner, said to be a Bay City resident. Lastly there was 50 year old Mary Shinske, the vessel's cook. Since 1899, Mary had been serving up the meals that fed the crews of assorted lake vessels. Without doubt she had long ago found the magic of preparing a variety of meals, with the minimum of provisions and accommodations. It was a background that served her well, in the cramped one-pot galley of the old wooden schooner-barge. All three of these people probably made up the stable element of the CRANE's crew, those who surely would be around for the whole season.

About the same time as Mary was putting the final touches on the crew's supper, the steamer HETTLER was pulling the CRANE off of Pigeon Bay and onto open Lake Superior. Back in the CRANE's pilothouse, located directly behind the boat's aft deck house, Captain Briggs was keeping a close watch ahead through the twin windows.

This was a route that the two boats had run many times in all kinds of weather. Ahead across the CRANE's deck-load, he could see the HETTLER producing bountiful smoke that the fresh wind was ripping from her funnel and dissolving across the lake. Their route would take the two boats due south past the western tip of Isle Royal, cutting between Fisherman's Reef and the Rock of Ages light. Once clear of these hazardous obstacles, they would haul east, southeast on a bee-line course for Whitefish Point. Passing down the Saint Mary's River, they would navigate the Straits of Mackinac and down Lake Michigan for Muskegon. Checking his pilothouse clock, Captain Briggs calculated they should be unloading some time late Friday or early Saturday. . . weather permitting.

Launched in 1881 at the David Lester Shipyard in Marine City, Michigan, the CRANE was originally christened as the THEO. S. FASSETT, making her living with sails hoisted upon three tall masts and the winds as power. However, she was born in the decline of sail-powered transportation and often found herself tagging along behind a tug or steamer, to make a profit. Measuring 199 feet in length and 32 feet across her beam with a reasonable 14 feet in depth, the boat was found to be exactly the right size for the schooner-barge concept. For the better placement of deck loads, her center mast was removed and she was left with only a single storm sail on the foremast, and pressed into the lumber trade. In 1918 she was re-named J.L. CRANE, and found herself part of the Blodgett lumber flotilla.

No sooner had the two Blodgett boats set out across Lake Superior than the gales of November set upon them. From out of the northwest the winds came suddenly booming at forces nearing 30 miles per hour. By morning the CRANE and HETTLER were taking quite a beating as the winds gusted over 50 miles per hour and the seas began to tower around the two small lakers. Taking the seas on their sterns, the lumber boats were being boarded by waves that began to leave ice on their hulls. Sometime during the day Wednesday, Captain Briggs ordered two of the crew out, to chip loose the CRANE's storm sail and raise it to the wind, hoping to help the HETTLER get the schooner-barge through the waves.

There were many other lakeboats caught up in the maelstrom, that fitful Thursday, funnelling toward Whitefish Bay. The steel trust 600 footers EUGENE W. PARGNY, and PETER A.B. WIDNER along with the 569 footer GEORGE W. PERKINS, were punching their way through the storm at different points across western Lake Superior. For these monsters of the 1920's the blow was rough going, but nothing more than they had gone through before. In the easternmost expanse of the lake another boat, who should have been making headway, was at the mercy of the gale. Bound out of Fort William, Ontario on the north shore, the Northern Navigation Company's 365 foot steel passenger steamer HAMONIC was bound for the Soo. Abruptly her engine surged, and almost immediately the steamer began to hang-up in the sea trough, while losing forward way. In minutes, she was rolling madly—in a manner that quickly had her passengers terrified.

Down in the HAMONIC's engine room her chief and engine crew scrambled about in a fruitless effort to determine the problem. Her engine had steam, her propeller shaft turned and her steering equipment functioned, but the HAMONIC just would not make headway. Below in her cargo hold, the odds and ends of packaged freight that she was carrying began to break loose with the rolling of the boat, and soon formed a sliding cascade back and forth across the deck. In the HAMONIC's pilothouse, Captain Montgomery ordered a distress signal sent from the boat's wireless. His position was sent out as just west, northwest of Caribou Island, and he had seas breaking completely over the vessel.

It seemed the boat had dropped into that abyss where tormented vessels go to be forever battered by Lake Superior when they sail through that fabled "crack in the lake" and are never seen again. To the souls aboard the HAMONIC it was as if they had already perished, and were now in a frigid, rolling black limbo. When all appeared lost, the HAMONIC's radio cries for relief seemed answered the lights of the 524 foot oreboat G.A. THOMLINSON materialized from the night. A stiletto beam of white light darted from the oreboat's spotlight and probed the helpless passenger-liner. Life-belted passengers crowded the HAMONIC's rails, as the vessel's dark hull rolled drunkenly in a monstrous sea. This was far more than the crew of the THOMLINSON had expected to encounter. If the HAMONIC decided to founder on the spot, the churning lake would become a sea of corpses in no time at all. The weather and seas were far too ferocious to render any kind of assistance to the HAMONIC, rolling so severely. At best the big oreboat could only stand by and wait for the worst, but that option soon vanished. Breaking hard over the THOMLINSON's stern and rampaging across her spar deck, the seas smashed at the hatch covers. The waters found her cargo hold and the THOMLINSON began to take on a list. Her captain had no option, beyond calling for full ahead on her chadburn and running for shelter behind Whitefish Point. Unhappily, the HAMONIC was once again left to her own ends, nearly due south of Caribou Island.

About this time some 40 miles south, southwest of the HAMONIC's plight, the HETTLER and CRANE were clawing their way across Boatswain Janssens' view. Having made his calls to the Vermillion Point station and dutifully expressed his open concern for the distant vessels,

Janssens turned his attention to the station log, and other chores. He should have felt lucky for having been spared the trauma of knowing what happened shortly after he glanced away from the two boats. As he turned his attention away, the lake was shoving the HETTLER's deck load overboard. To make matters worse, the steamer was taking a huge amount of water into her hold—it seemed the end was but a short time away. So grim was the situation, the HETTLER's crew had donned their life jackets, in preparation for the deadly meeting with Lake Superior.

One of the steamer's firemen, Fred Zinn, had put his life jacket on and was helping with pumping operations, in an effort to control the flooding. He was on his way up the companionway when the HETTLER abruptly lurched beneath his feet. The violent movement was accompanied by the defining moans and snapping of shattered timbers, as if the boat was pulling itself apart. For an instant Zinn must have thought that this must be what it is like when your boat founders, and not wanting to be trapped inside, he scrambled for the open deck. As he bursted through the door without a breath, a second series of exploding timber sounds drew his eyes to the stern rail. Frozen for a moment, the terrified fireman had turned aft just in time to witness the HETTLER's giant tow-post being ripped from the deck. A sizable portion of the steamer's deck went with the post as it vanished into the blackness. With a bursting roar, the after cabin behind Zinn was saturated with white steam, as the lights in the HETTLER's stern flickered out. In the distance behind, he saw the dim masthead lights of the CRANE for a second—before they suddenly vanished.

No time was available to worry about the schooner-barge. The HETTLER was badly wounded, all hands would be needed to save her. The ripping away of her tow-post had wrecked a big chunk of the dining room floor, not to mention a sizeable portion of the stern decking. Every wave that mounted the stern sent cascades of Lake Superior through the yawning cavity, and down to the lower decks. When the tow-post was extracted it ruptured a steam line, knocking out the frail electrical system in the stern. Odds are that the engine crew felt much the same as the HAMONIC's souls, as if they had been banished to the netherworld itself. In the blackness of the engine room, their shovels heaved coal using only the fires that it stoked for illumination. Loose steam saturated every opening, the deck pitched insanely beneath their feet and rolling waves of sooty, intruding water sloshed hip-deep. Shovel they did, shoveling for the survival of their boat, shoveling for Whitefish Point, shoveling for their lives.

When he felt the CRANE let go, the HETTLER's master began blowing his whistle, to attract the attention of the Crisp Point or Vermillion Point stations. But standing on the shore less than 5000 feet from the HETTLER, Tom Singleton heard nothing. Turning the steamer to back-track to the CRANE, with the gash the HETTLER now had in her stern, was completely out of the question. His best bet was to run at full steam for the point and after ducking behind it, try to contact the Whitefish Point station.

Just what it was in the hull timbers of the HETTLER that allowed her to survive the 15 odd mile grapple to the shelter of Whitefish Bay, will never be known. Perhaps it was the will of her crew to survive, the skill of the craftsmen at the Davidson Shipyard in 1890, or just plain Providence, the steamer hauled around the point and into protected waters, thwarting Lake Superior. Once in shelter, several crew members volunteered to take a lifeboat and attempt a row to the Whitefish Point station, to alert the Coast Guard to the plight of both boats. Their effort, unfortunately, was beaten back by the storm after making only a short distance, and the volunteers were forced to pull back for the HETTLER. After stabilizing the situation aboard his boat, the HETTLER's master ordered steam up again, and the wounded laker limped for the Soo.

Friday morning revealed the scarred steamer tied to the Brady Pier, and throughout the day several battered lakers joined the HETTLER in breathing a collective sigh of relief. Feeling beaten, the THOMLINSON skulked into port with a three foot list and several collapsed hatches. The ROBERT J. PAISLEY came limping in with her deck load pillaged, after cabins smashed, yawl boat plucked away and water in her coal bunker. To the relief of all, the big steel 600 footer RICHARD TRIMBLE steamed triumphantly into the Soo, the HAMONIC safely in tow. (A subsequent investigation revealed that the passenger steamer's giant bronze propeller had come loose and fallen off in mid-lake, leaving her helpless.)

Like a firestorm, news of the wreckage thought to be from the CRANE, spread through the Soo. During the day the word went out that Captain McLeod of the PETER A.B. WIDENER had spotted a drifting yawl near the tip of Whitefish Point, and that it was of the kind used on barges like the CRANE. Many took this as the concluding evidence that the barge had foundered, taking her crew with her. It is more likely that the yawl was the one plucked from the PAISLEY, since the wreckage washed up on shore contained a piece of the smashed yawl from the CRANE. The CRANE's flotsam field also stopped nearly four miles west of Whitefish Point, and considering the gale was heavy from the northwest, the yawl that Captain McLeod had spotted was probably not from the schooner-barge. Fireman Zinn's account of the barge breaking loose was picked up by local papers, together with his speculation that the barge had capsized.

For two more full days the gale raged relentlessly, easing up late Saturday. Joe Singleton and another of the

A once-active sailing boat, the J.L. CRANE was forced out of wind power and onto the end of a towing hawser. With the aid of a consort steamer, she worked well into the 1920s.

Crisp Point keepers then went out in a small boat, powered by a five horsepower motor, to try and locate the CRANE. They found only a bobbing spar broken from the barge, and putting a line on it, dragged it back to the station. Later, about three feet of the butt of the white pine spar was cut off, and served for many years as a meat chopping block at the station. The rest was cut up for firewood.

At dawn Monday, the Coast Guard cutter COOK set out to search for the missing CRANE. The search did not take long. At 11 o'clock the cutter came upon a shattered spar tethered to the bottom—just one mile off Crisp Point station, in 24 feet of water. Not far away, the stern rail of the schooner-barge could be glimpsed between the swells. Returning to the Soo the Coast Guardsmen issued an advisory to vessels, that the wreck posed a menace to navigation for those using the shore route. Four days later, the lighthouse tender MARIGOLD went to the wreck to place a buoy on it, but when the tender arrived, they found only a floating spar and boom-held in place by tangled rigging. The rest of the CRANE was nowhere to be seen.

Lake Superior never gave up the bodies of the J.L. CRANE's crew. As of this writing, it has never given up the schooner-barge either. Research divers, including members of the Great Lakes Shipwreck Historical Society, have searched for the schooner-barge, but Superior's sandy bottom has yet to yield as much as a timber. In the six fathom water, where the boat supposedly went down, it is common for winter's ice to grind right down to the bottom, and for autumn and spring gales to shift the sands— enough to swallow a small house. The chances are that the barge was broken up within a season or three, and the remains covered over by roving sand, buried forever in one of Lake Superior's unmarked graves.

So just what did happen to the CRANE? The absolute answer to that is known only to those who went down with her, but by using some of the reported information, a plausible description of the event can be constructed. What is paramount in this speculation are the two lost deck loads and their being washed up on shore together, the shattered yawl, the ripped out tow-post, the depth of the water, the over-the-bottom speed of the two boats, the floating spar that Joe Singleton found, the sand bottom and, lastly, the finding of the wreck with its stern rail showing above the surface. A few important facts too about the boat's configuration have to be accounted for. Her yawl was mounted at the stern rail, she carried two spars, but only the forward one was equipped with a boom, and her mast head lights were mounted about 60 feet from the deck on that forward spar.

In review of the accounts of the day, both boats were making no headway, and the HETTLER was swept by a sea great enough to put her deckload over the side and set her to leaking. Then the tow-post was torn out and shortly thereafter the lights of the CRANE, as seen from the steamer, went out. But according to Tom Singleton, the CRANE's lights vanished all at once from his shore side perspective.

With this in hand, we can put together a possible scenario. Coming across Crisp Point the two boats, making no headway, are overtaken by an unusually large wave sending most of their deck loads over. If this wave set the HETTLER to leaking, there is a strong possibility that the CRANE, nine years older, may have been suffering from a similar intrusion at this time, if not sooner. Shortly, the schooner-barge would be so waterlogged that one of the big waves lifts her stern and she takes a nose dive, driving her bow into the sandy bottom. The combination of the dive, mixed with the HETTLER's forward power, tugs the tow-post from the steamer. Fireman Zinn is in a position to see only the masthead light which, although the schooner-barge is already on the bottom, is still slightly above the surface. From Tom Singleton's perspective, however, the cabin lights are best seen, and go out, as the schooner dives. Submerged with her bow impaled in the sand, and stern nearly on the surface, the CRANE is hit by the next wave—which smashes her yawl against the now stationary wreck, takes down the stern mast and plucks away the remaining light on the foremast. Mostly submerged, the foremast with its boom lasts for several more days before breaking loose, but the aft mast is discovered shortly after the wreck.

All of this is nothing more than speculation and the actual facts are few. What is certain is that in that three day storm of November, 1925, seven souls were lost to

One of the last of the wooden lumber hookers, the HERMAN H. HETTLER would work only one year beyond her battle with Lake Superior while towing the J.L. CRANE. A year and 21 days after Superior swallowed the CRANE, it would claim the HETTLER as well.

Lake Superior. Four of these luckless individuals will forever remain anonymous, their names never recorded. One year later, nearly to the day the HETTLER herself would find her end, just 67 miles from the CRANE's unmarked grave. In the decade of the 1920s, the Blodgett fleet seemed the place where wooden vessels went to die. From 1920 to 1929 a dozen Blodgett boats were wrecked on the lakes. It was as if Mr. Blodgett's signature on a vessel's papers was indeed one of misfortune.

Today, all of the buildings that once made up the Crisp Point station, with the exception of the lighthouse itself, are gone. Lake Superior has reclaimed most of the land on which the buildings once stood, and the structures that once housed the Singleton men have been dismantled.

And each autumn and spring gale brings a marauding surf, that eats at the beach and may soon undermine the lighthouse. Inevitably, the entire setting in which the J.L. CRANE took her final bow will be pulverized by Superior's winter ice flows and covered by her shifting sands. Only the mighty lake itself will remain. Fortunately, at the time of this writing, Tom Singleton is still around . . . and remembers that deplorable night when his dad sent him out to set the sticks in front of the Crisp Point station. Speaking as if it were yesterday, he tells this story of that night in 1925 for he has the distinction of being the only eyewitness, to the sinking of the J.L. CRANE . . .

Captain Oliver's
Extended Season

*F*or Captain Joseph Oliver the third week of October, 1901 had turned out to be a bright spot in what had been an otherwise sour autumn. As the good captain peered from the rail of the passenger steamer CHARLES H. HACKLEY, there appeared a bit more twinkle in his eye. Easing through the narrow channel, the HACKLEY hissed into the port-lake of Muskegon, Michigan arriving from Chicago with her passengers and bringing Captain Oliver, not as master, but as a passenger. The word had come down from Managing Owner Miles F. Barry that the steamer STATE OF MICHIGAN was to be brought out of lay-up and Captain Oliver was to take command of her pilothouse. It is more desirable to command than to play second fiddle on someone else's boat, and so what if the STATE OF MICHIGAN had seen better days, she would be Captain Oliver's charge and that was good enough for him. Unknown to the good captain, as well as Mr. Barry, the elderly STATE OF MICHIGAN was about to earn her owners a tidy $11,000—in a way that none of them could foresee.

Muskegon itself is probably one of the best natural harbors on Lake Michigan. The port is in reality a large lake at the end of the Muskegon River, that formed directly adjacent to Lake Michigan. Oddly, in 1779 when H.M.S. FELICITY was making her expedition along Lake Michigan's shores, Captain Samuel Robertson decided to put in at this natural harbor, expecting to find the normal mix of trappers and Indians. The Englishman was startled to find instead a black man dominating trading pursuits at the lake-harbor. In a time when the entire settled United States, as well as parts not yet colonized, was a domain of black slavery, the man who Robertson referred to simply as "Black Peter," was freely going about his trade. Questioning conversation later revealed Black Peter was just one of a group who were established and making a living at assorted sites along the Lake Michigan shore and up toward Mackinaw. Apparently no one had ever told Black Peter that emancipation was nearly 100 years away. That mattered little, for in the wilderness around lake Michigan in the 1700s, everyone was free without regard to color. It was courage and skill that counted, and it is evident that Black Peter and his contemporaries, who had eluded the chains of slavery and made their place in the wilderness, had an ample supply of both.

There is no record as to what became of Black Peter or the rest of his fellow un-slaves, as the town of Muskegon was about to boom, and men like him merely retreated deeper into the shrinking wilderness, because it alone was their freedom. Lumber was the fuel that supported the town's boom, lumber cut from the surrounding dense forests that had freed Black Peter—cut and floated down the mighty Muskegon River and milled in the town named for the river. In 1887 some 665,000,000 board feet of lumber were milled, at the zenith of the town's boom. But the lumber production declined steeply as the surrounding forests were depleted to a near moonscape. By the time the HACKLEY plodded into port in 1901 the scene was one of almost total economic blight. Sawmills, 47 in number, sat rusting and abandoned. Planked sidewalks and bricked streets led between vacated wooden buildings, demonstrating what happens when an industry dies and its workers are uprooted.

Resting at an out-of-the-way slip in the harbor of Muskegon, the STATE OF MICHIGAN seemed to be patiently waiting to return to work. Hers had been a long and highly lucrative career, starting with her initial enrollment on the 25th day of July, 1873. Launched from the Rand and Burger yard at Manitowoc, Wisconsin, the STATE OF MICHIGAN was one of a common class of combination package and passenger propellers used on the Great Lakes. Her hull was constructed of oak timbers and measured 165 feet in overall length, 29 feet in beam and 20 feet in depth, displacing 736 tons. An official number of 6849 was assigned with the vessel's U.S. registration, and she was christened DE PERE to begin her career. The boat's configuration was much the same as others engaged in the same passenger and cargo trade. The cargo was taken aboard through side ports, and her passengers were carried one deck above, in cabins rivaling the passenger trains of the era. Her sea trials complete, the DE PERE was pressed into the Goodrich Line on their Lake Michigan routes.

In April 1893 Vesselman Stephen B. Grummond purchased the DE PERE, and on the 10th day of that month he re-christened her STATE OF MICHIGAN. Interestingly, the boat's records show a "rebuild" at the time, but the only listed change was a four-inch increase in length! For about the next five seasons the STATE OF MICHIGAN ran for Mister Grummond from Detroit to various Lake Huron ports. By 1898, however, the wooden steamer was showing her age and Grummond saw fit to put her up for sale. Chicago's Barry brothers offered the meager sum of $19,000 for the vessel's purchase, and their offer was promptly accepted by their Detroit counterpart, thus sending the STATE OF MICHIGAN back onto the Lake Michigan routes. For the better part of the next two years, the lethargic old steamer pounded between Chicago and

Muskegon, under the flag of the Chicago and Muskegon Transportation Company.

Early in 1901 the Barrys acquired the iron passenger propeller HARTFORD from the U.S. Army Quartermaster Corps, and brought her from salt water service to Lake Michigan, where she was renamed CHARLES H. HACKLEY, and assigned to the STATE OF MICHIGAN's route. As a direct result of the new steamer's arrival, the venerable STATE OF MICHIGAN was sent to the lay-up wall, where she remained until Captain Oliver got his sailing orders. The wooden steamer's salvation as a charter, to carry salt from Manistee, Michigan to Chicago—and from the word Captain Oliver had heard from the front office, it sounded like there would be plenty of work until the season's end.

A crew of 12 had been hired by the Messrs. Barry to staff the STATE OF MICHIGAN, including Captain Oliver. Bound from Chicago were First Mate O.E. Hogobum, Chief Engineer M. Burns, wheelsmen William Eddy and John Duffler, watchman Frank Newell and firemen William Septon and William Murphy. Other members of the crew were already in Muskegon, being locals. Acting as second engineer was Muskegon resident Rudolph Drum and wheeling in the STATE OF MICHIGAN's pilothouse would be August Person, while working the galley was fellow Muskegonite Fred Rabel. Only cook Star Foot was not from Muskegon or Chicago, having been hired out of Milwaukee. By Thursday night the whole crew had been mustered, and the STATE OF MICHIGAN was alive once more and nearing readiness for an early morning departure.

For the better part of a week, Chief Burns and his second had been struggling with the vessel's engineworks. It must have seemed the STATE OF MICHIGAN's machinery was an unending assembly of rusting, leaking devices. Leaving any vessel at the wall is hard on the equipment, but an antiquated wooden steamer such as this was particularly vulnerable to the lay-up gremlins. Chief Burns had, by the night before the vessel sailed, managed to evict all of the gremlins that he could find. The rest of them would have to be exorcised while underway.

At the first hints of daylight on Friday October 18th, 1901 the big propeller on the ancient steamer churned to life again. Accumulated silt from the boat's protracted lay-up swirled from her submerged hull timbers, as the STATE OF MICHIGAN wriggled back to work. At first, her equipment groaned in protest with each movement, but soon the boat was fully awakened and on her way to work. The first leg of the trip would be a relatively short steam up the Michigan shore to the town of Manistee, where her cargo of Chicago-bound barreled salt waited. The weather was surprisingly moderate for mid-October, and Captain Oliver thought to be at the Manistee entrance about nine hours after clearing Muskegon. If loading was completed by midday Saturday, he could have the STATE OF MICHIGAN underway in short order, and perhaps into Chicago by about the same time the following day.

Down in the boat's engine room, the situation was different, with Chief Burns waging unending battle with countless glitches. Steam escaped from where it should not, bearings required additional oil and the engine produced noises that most do not—maybe there were a few more demons in residence than the chief had calculated. Like his counterpart in the pilothouse, Chief Burns was determined to keep his boat working since it was far better than working as a second engineer on another of the company's steamers.

Snoring through the Muskegon channel, the STATE OF MICHIGAN pushed a couple of miles onto Lake Michigan, and Captain Oliver ordered her hauled over on the right wheel and pointed for Little Sable Point some 31 miles up the coast. Aft in the galley, the two cooks were getting breakfast underway because as soon as the captain got his boat settled in, he was apt to think about strolling aft for a bite. The galley on the STATE OF MICHIGAN was exceptionally large compared to most lakers with only a crew of 12, because it had been designed to accommodate several dozen passengers, as well as the crew. Her passenger quarters stood empty and smelling of sun-baked must, the beds stripped and the fixtures in a hollow jumble like an abandoned vacation cabin. Elbow room aplenty was one blessing that the two cooks had bestowed on them, although the odds are that the galley had been stocked only with minimal provisions, just enough to get her crew to Chicago, where company stores were available.

Just as the crotchety steamer came abeam White Lake, only 11 miles up the coast from Muskegon, there was a dull bang that echoed from deep within the boat. The sound was that of cannon fire hitting the boat, and steam erupted from every opening at the old lakeboat's stern. For a moment, Captain Oliver probably reckoned that the boat had burst a steam line, but there was something about the odd sound that alarmed him—it was a noise like none he had heard before. Next came the distant rattling and thumping of loose machinery. The boat's steam was vented overboard and the STATE OF MICHIGAN slowed to a stop.

From the pilothouse, the captain sent Mate Hogobum back to the engine room to find out what in blazes happened. As the mate made his way down into the firehold, he found the engine crew wallowing about in rising water. Shouts and swear words echoed through the filthy steam-saturated air, as everyone scrambled around. Working his way back to the engine, he found the chief up to his elbows in a giant mound of gushing water. Without doubt the chief made the situation crystal clear to the mate, in

Seen here doing battle with the lake, the steamer STATE OF MICHIGAN seems happy at work. After falling on idle days, however, she was given another chance to find her place among workin' boats—instead she found the bottom of Lake Michigan.

very few words. The STATE OF MICHIGAN's engine had broken a connecting rod and shot one of its big pistons, like an artillery shell, right through the bottom of the boat.

His soaked feet slinging water ahead, Mate Hogobum dashed back to the pilothouse. Moments later, Captain Oliver decided that his boat was in danger of sinking and began blowing the whistle, in an effort to use what steam remained to attract the attention of the life savers at White River. But the situation was far worse than the captain first thought, for there was absolutely no way to plug the nearly three foot hole in the boat's bottom. The pumps lacked the steam to operate and soon the water was bursting in, to the point where the engine crew were driven from their stations, like so many rats. Totally disabled, the STATE OF MICHIGAN was sinking and nothing could stop her.

At the stern, the crew began to gather rags, sheets, mattresses and anything else that would burn, saturating the pile with oil and igniting the whole mound. This too was an effort to attract attention from shore. The effort was a success, for the tug McGRAFF soon huffed out of the port, and aboard were the White River lifesavers. As the tug eased alongside the floundering steamer, a line was hastily made secure between the two. The crew of the STATE OF MICHIGAN were transferred and the tug-of-war to beach was on.

Watching from the tug's stern, the dozen men of the STATE OF MICHIGAN watched helplessly as the steamer began losing its race with the lake. Steadily the steamer's stern began to be consumed by Lake Michigan, until it was threatening to take the tug with her. Sadly, the line to the STATE OF MICHIGAN was let go and the crowd aboard the tug witnessed the steamer passing out of service forever. Chugging back to White Lake, the tug dropped the castaways off at the town of Montague, so that they could make their way back to Muskegon. By mid-day, Miles Barry had a telegram on his desk stating that the old steamer had been lost, but all aboard were safe.

Four days after the sinking, the steamer's enrollment was surrendered at Chicago and endorsed simply "vessel lost." Interestingly, the Barry brothers had the old vessel insured for $20,000, but reported her value as being $30,000. Not bad considering that they bought her for $19,000, ran her two years, stripped her accommodations and laid her up. Somewhere in the process her value increased by $11,000, or at least that is what the Barrys claimed. To what benefit this was is anyone's guess, but for such a valuable asset, the boat was just left to the elements in less than 70 feet of water, easily within the reach of the hard-hat divers of the day. No attempt at salvage was ever made, and the STATE OF MICHIGAN was forgotten where she lay two miles off the beach at White Lake.

Today, all of the players in the STATE OF MICHIGAN's tale have passed from existence. The passage of time has left behind all of the boat's crew, her owners have folded their business, and their concerns have long been forgotten—and it has been decades since the last of the big passenger and freight steamers ceased crisscrossing Lake Michigan. The winter ice has smashed the remains of the STATE OF MICHIGAN into nothing more than a few shattered timbers and some twisted engine machinery, all occasionally covered by wandering sand. So powerful are the ice-floes that even the steamer's massive boilers have been beaten down, bitter evidence that the lake has more time and more power than man or his devices. Like so many vessels in Great Lakes history, the memory of the steamer STATE OF MICHIGAN withered away as quickly as Captain Oliver's expectation of a gainful end to the 1901 season. This is not surprising considering that Captain Oliver's extended season had ended prematurely, and unquestionably, with a bang.

Touring the area surrounding Muskegon, there is little evidence that an all-consuming lumber industry had stripped the land to a desert. Nature has replaced much of the forests that were clear-cut, and the river is now used for floating canoes loaded with summer vacationers, instead of logs to be milled. The harbor-lake, once the waiting place for retiring wooden passenger liners, is now the port of occasional lakers, tugs and fishing boats. Drifting past the cabins and deep green woods, the users of the Muskegon River should listen and look carefully, for they just may catch the image of Black Peter, who forever lives among the dense woods that kept him free. When departing the harbor-lake that makes up the port at the end of the river, the coho fishermen may be tempted to turn north and trace the route of Captain Oliver. That blob that appears on the fish-finder, just over a dozen miles north of Muskegon, two miles off shore and in 70 feet of water, is the sad remains of the steamer that cut the captain's extended season short—but still earned her owners a neat $11,000 in profit by conveniently sinking to the bottom of Lake Michigan . . . and staying there forever.

Mute Evidence

*W*orriedly, James Swift tapped a pencil atop his desk, trying not to look at the leaden autumn sky outside of his Kingston, Ontario office. He was the boss, and at times like this the greater portion of worry was rightfully his to bear. At bigger companies, such concerns had been felt before, but this was the first time this sort of atmosphere had hung over the firm of Swift and Sons. It was Tuesday afternoon, the 23rd of September, 1919 and all the anxiety was centered around a dwarfish steamer and the marginal cargo of coal that she carried for her owners, the Swifts. As the clock prepared to strike three, Mr. Swift decided it was time to begin telephoning the various Lake Ontario ports in an attempt to find some trace of his missing boat. After all, she was nearly 16 hours overdue.

A day and a half before Mr. Swift's trembling hand picked up the telephone, an insignificant little steam-scow tied up under the Fair Haven, New York coal trestle, on the southern shore of Lake Ontario and nearly directly across from Kingston. In the wake of the larger canal class steamers that took coal from this same dock at two or three thousand tons per load, the 249 tons to be loaded aboard the tiny T.J. WAFFLE, seemed hardly worth the manpower for the loading rig. But when Captain Beaupre left the WAFFLE and entered the dock office, that was exactly the amount he ordered. Odds are that the diminutive steamer could not hold much more than that and remain afloat.

Born at the waterside town of Westport, Ontario in 1914, the WAFFLE was the handiwork of Joseph Paradis. He had been contracted by the Waffle brothers, William and Walter, to construct a vessel for hauling assorted cargos around Big Lake Rideau and up the Rideau River to Ottawa. For such work a vessel of shallow draft would be required, allowing it to slide up to docks of the resort towns, where little depth of water was common. The boat also must be of a size and shape that would allow passage through the canal, outside of the city of Ottawa. Paradis' solution to the design problems was to build the hull in the shape of a scow barge—with a flat-bottomed rectangular hull, a square stern and slightly sloped bow. At the stern he mounted a simple deck house and booth-like pilothouse. For the long hauls up the Rideau, a cramped but functional galley and Spartan crew quarters were installed. A meager steam engine was planted at the stern, just enough to amble her along the peaceful waterway at a sleepy five to six miles per hour. Her hold had no hatches or hatch covers, because there was no need. The boat would work where the biggest seas would be in the range of a foot or two, so why obstruct her hold with hatches? When his toil was over, Paradis had constructed a wooden steamer of scow build that displaced 202 tons and measured 112 feet in length by 22 feet in beam and just eight feet in depth. It was just what the Waffle brothers wanted.

When Walter Waffle took possession of the steamer he decided to christen it with the name of his pride and joy, his 15 year old son Thomas John Waffle. Young Thomas had taken a great interest in his father and uncle's business and was currently enthusiastically employed by his elders, probably doing as many of the menial tasks as could be created by his kin. Considering his current interest in the Waffles' livelihood, there seemed no better way to insure the boy would follow in the family footsteps than to name a steamboat after him. Thus the T.J. WAFFLE went to work. On her sea trials across Big Lake Rideau, no doubt her giddy 15 year old namesake spent time at the wheel, as his father and uncle looked on. Surely such a golden moment should be the prelude to many happy days to come.

World events tended to race far beyond the grasp of those who ran the Waffle family business, and would suddenly make that great day in 1914 a special memory amid tragic times. In the same year as the WAFFLE was launched, the nation of Canada had joined its counterpart in Great Britain, in the great war against the German Huns. In less than two years, Thomas Waffle, not yet 17 years of age, signed up to go over seas and fight for his country. Before the first spring breeze of 1916 blustered, Walter Waffle received a telegram that his pride, his son, had been killed in action in France on the 16th day of March.

Perhaps he just no longer had the will to press on with the family business as it was, or perhaps the Rideau trade was just not working out. Whatever the reason, the Waffle family business began to fade. Unquestionably the little steamer revived Walter Waffle's pain each time he saw her, the nameboard alone was mute evidence of his personal loss. Shortly after his son's death the senior Waffle sold the steam-scow for $12,000 to the Swifts who had plans for her on the north shore of Lake Ontario. For the last time, she was sailed from the Rideau waters, down to Lake Ontario and the port city of Kingston. Doubtless there were times when Mr. Waffle could hear the steamer's familiar whistle from his Kingston home, or he would spot her around the city's waterfront. What thoughts and memories such encounters brought were his alone to shoulder.

There were many elegant vessels constructed for Great Lakes service in the first two decades of the 1900s. From the giant, steel-hulled oreboats that made the long hauls to the massive car ferries that crushed ice to navigate year round, there were scores of outstanding examples of the shipbuilder's art working the freshwater seas. With this impressive machinery constantly moving in and out of the lake ports, it would be easy to overlook a vessel such as the WAFFLE. She was somewhat unremarkable in size and appearance, and definitely not constructed for use out across the open lake. From no matter what angle the mariners observed the steam-scow, she was not at all pretty but certainly one of a kind. In truth, she was an odd duck among the Lake Ontario boats.

To Captain Beaupre, the WAFFLE was a tool of hard work and not a kind of "odd duck," as many viewed her. For the job that the Swifts had engaged her, the little steamer had performed quite efficiently. Her task was to pick up small loads of coal on the southern Lake Ontario shore and haul it back to Kingston. Normally these burdens of fossil fuel were loaded at either Fair Haven or Oswego, and with good weather the round trip could be made in just over 24 hours. The result was coal could be brought up in marginal quantities, at marginal rates.

Choosing a boat such as the WAFFLE was no easy task. The Swifts were concerned with the cost of running the operation, meaning minimum pay for maximum work. The result was that those who served aboard the boat were transients- at best. So, on that gloomy Monday morning in October 1919, there was no record of the names and details of the WAFFLE's people. Aside from her captain, the sole crewmember who was on record as being aboard, was Marshell Switzer who was known to reside at 277 Ontario street with his wife and family, when he was not sailing. Switzer was signed aboard as a fireman, and was one of the few who had been aboard for any length of time. There was too a new lady cook who had come aboard with her husband, employed as a crewman of some sort. Both of these nameless individuals had come aboard at Kingston a few days earlier. For the rest of the crew, there was no need for the Swifts to make or retain records of their names. The fact was that crewmen were paid in cash, and came and went so frequently that it was nearly impossible to keep track of them. So, when the first rumblings of coal tumbled into the WAFFLE's scanty hold, nobody, other than those aboard, knew exactly who her crew was, or even how many were aboard.

It took just a short time for the WAFFLE to take aboard her 249 tons of coal. Just after 10 a.m. on Monday, the little steam-scow pushed silently from the harbor of Fair Haven and out onto Lake Ontario, largely ignored by nearly everyone. Her hull weighed down by several small hills of the rocks that burn and funnel belching thick billows of smoke, the WAFFLE was obviously starting a hard day's work with her normal determination to get the job done. By noon, the bantam lakeboat was little more than a smudge of coal smoke on the gray horizon.

That same morning, a modest autumn wind came lofting down from the province of Ontario, blowing across the lake and kicking up a nasty chop. Around mid-afternoon, the winds were increasing from nearly due north and were approaching storm force. Downbound for the port of Oswego came the tug MUSCALONGE of the Sin Mac line, with the wind at her heels. From the tug's pilothouse, vigilant eyes spotted another vessel plowing north, northeast into the whitecaps. In the distance, it was easy to identify the steamer as the WAFFLE—after all, she was one of a kind. At the time, the tug's crew took little notice of the tiny steam-scow, but the captain did note the time as being half past five in the evening. Shortly, the tug's skipper observed the distant vessel turn from a north-bound course to a south-bound heading, apparently heading for a south shore port.

Into the night, the autumn winds huffed and clouds lowered and darkened around the port of Kingston. By daylight the sky painted the backdrop for an ugly day to come. Making his normal early morning arrival at his office, Mr. Swift set about his routine. A call to the dock where the WAFFLE's cargo was consigned was in order, but the dock foreman notified the vessel owner that the boat had not yet arrived. She had been due around midnight but, considering the weather, there was no cause for alarm. The little boat was ill equipped to handle any kind of sea, so it was likely that Captain Beaupre had decided to seek shelter. Perhaps the WAFFLE was at that moment squatting behind the Duck Islands or Prince Edward Point, waiting for daylight before running the last few miles into Kingston. Then again, the captain may have run her out onto the lake until late Monday and, not liking the looks of things, run south into Oswego to spend the night.

By three o'clock in the afternoon, Mr. Swift's concern had grown to near panic. For a long time he had put off making a telephone search, hoping that no news was good news, but now he had to know. The winds had died to a breeze shortly after sunrise and the WAFFLE was seriously overdue. If the boat had sheltered behind one of the northeast islands or Prince Edward Point she was, at worst, six hours steaming time from Kingston. If she had put into Oswego, Captain Beaupre would certainly have phoned the office to give word of his delay. On his call to Oswego, Mr. Swift got the information that he most feared—the WAFFLE had not come into port. Also, he was informed that the wreckage of a wooden steamer was currently washing ashore from west of Beach Oswego to Lake Ontario Park, and had been doing so since before dawn. Although he tried to hold out hope, Mr. Swift knew in his heart that his worst fears had come to pass. His little steamer was gone.

Shortly after the first of the flotsam had been reported coming ashore, Captain Clemons of the Oswego Coast Guard station and Ship Chandler John S. Parsons set out to patrol the beach and attempt to gather what they could. Their efforts recovered seven life preservers, with the name "T.J. WAFFLE" stenciled on them. Soon large sections of her deck house washed up, one piece having a fire axe fastened securely, where it had hung when the ill-fated boat was still alive. There were mattresses, pillows, oars and shattered lifeboat davits that found their way to the beach. Significantly, the boat's steering wheel came in with about 100 feet of chain still attached. Apparently, whatever happened to the WAFFLE had completely torn her apart. The evening saw the winds shift to the south, and thereafter Lake Ontario kept everything else from the T.J. WAFFLE. Not a single body of any of her crew is known to have been recovered, only the giant pieces of the boat, mute evidence of the loss of the WAFFLE and her people.

So just what did happen to the paltry little steam-scow? The answer to that is known only to those who perished with her and to Lake Ontario itself. Conjecture at the time immediately speculated that the boat had exploded her boiler. Curiously, this theory was repeated over and over in the newspapers, a fact that is somewhat telling. The large pieces of wreckage that came ashore, the items that would have been located deep in her cabins and hull given up by the lake seemed to indicate an explosion. This was particularly true of the wheel and steering chain, which runs into the deepest part of a vessel's stern, like a tendon in one's body. Normally, when a wooden boat takes a nose-dive, even a violent plunge leaves the steering works with the wreck. The hull would have to have been blown into splinters to extricate the wheel and chain. Many of these "back yard built" steam engines were prone to boiler explosions when the systems were deprived of

There are no photos of the T.J. WAFFLE known to exist. We know only that she was "a steamer of scow-build," constructed for the Rideau River trade. The image presented here is strictly the author's impression of how she may have looked and was created from a photo of a similar vessel of the same era. Photos of vessels said to be the WAFFLE should be carefully considered before concluding that they are, in fact, the missing boat.

water, or the pressure was improperly monitored, or sometimes for seemingly no reason at all. Such incidents were seen in tugs constructed under the same circumstances as the WAFFLE, and worked a small crew much like the lost steam-scow.

The premise that the boat had foundered near to shore was also put out. This, on the assumption that the wreckage found the beach so quickly that the wreck must have been close to shore. This would seem to contradict the explosion supposition, because nobody in Oswego or the surrounding beach-side residences heard any kind of explosion. A boiler explosion which would shatter a steamer would have been of the caliber of a modern sonic boom and should have been heard for many miles around.

Exactly where out on Lake Ontario the crew of the tug MUSCALONGE spotted the WAFFLE is not recorded. This would facilitate matters in calculating the chain of events in the loss of the vessel. If she was making as little as five miles per hour in over-the-bottom speed, at half past five o'clock in the afternoon the boat would have been less than four miles below the shelter of Main Duck Island, which was into the wind from her course. So why turn to the south? The island's lee was less than an hour away, the southern ports were six hours off. But, if her over-the-bottom speed was reduced by the winds and seas by as little a factor as two miles per hour, the WAFFLE would have been pounding nearly at mid-lake. A turn to the south and a run before the waves would have been a logical maneuver. Which, if any, of these courses of action Captain Beaupre elected to use will remain unknown.

In no way was the little steam-scow constructed for the open lake, in any kind of storm. She was a river vessel and meant for nothing more. With a bit of imagination, we can see the WAFFLE, heavily loaded and low in the water, pushing onto Lake Ontario. With a modest sea running, the lake easily finds its way over her scow nose and into the yawning hold. Just before six o'clock in the evening, Captain Beaupre finds his boat, impeded severely by the wind and seas, barely half way across the lake and taking much water. His best bet is to turn and flee before the seas. The WAFFLE's deck house would give some shelter to the vulnerable cargo hold from the boarding waves and perhaps allow the pumps to catch up.

The end may have come in one of two ways—with her bow low from the water shipped into the cargo hold the scow could have put her nose into a wave and plunged toward the bottom, her red-hot boiler bursting as it met the frigid lake. The other possibility is that after turning the boat and giving the pumps their chance, Captain Beaupre chose to keep running to Oswego. With a crew of only seven or eight, including the captain and cook, every spare hand would have been preoccupied in pumping operations. It would not be hard to imagine the engineer being distracted from the gauges for just the wrong amount of time. Somewhere at that moment, perhaps just far enough out to be inaudible ashore, her boiler exploded—leveling the boat to the waterline.

Such musings on the hows and whys of the WAFFLE's loss are absolutely pure supposition, made more than eight decades after the loss. Even the physical evidence of the disaster has long since been swallowed by the passing years. What a modern historian would not give to be able to examine a plank, a shattered davit or any other piece of debris from a wreck such as the WAFFLE, in an effort to reason the loss. As of this writing, the wreck has not yet been discovered, and the boat's loss has even been overlooked by local residents. Even if it were found, would the divers recognize the shattered hull as being Captain Beaupre's lost command, or would they simply chalk it off as an old coal scow? The T.J. WAFFLE, you see, was quickly forgotten. Who would miss the little steam-scow in the din of Lake Ontario's maritime commerce? She had been on the big lake only for a couple of years, not long enough to be photographed—and certainly not long enough to be well-remembered.

All we can say for certain is that sometime between half past five on Monday evening September 22nd, 1919 and dawn the following day, a trivial steam-scow met a sudden and violent end somewhere off Oswego, and took seven or eight souls with her. The T.J. WAFFLE left behind only mute evidence of her end, which itself soon faded away. If she had been a more remarkable vessel, with a larger complement of crew, she might have been honored with the title of being one of the ghost ships of the lakes. Such was not to be the case, for the WAFFLE, like the young man that she had been named after, just died violently—and was swallowed into the eddy of obscure history. To those who research and exhume Great Lakes maritime history the little steamer appears on occasion and floats amid the yellowing pages, sometimes having her facts confused with incorrect photos, but being quickly lost among the shuffling papers once again. A true ghost ship of the history books . . .

What a Scoop!

*B*lissfully, Jim Mahony was sleeping away the early hours of the third Monday in October, 1950. Outside the bedroom window of his residence at 3319 Reid Ave in Lorain, Ohio, the winds were whipping at the sill in a vain attempt to gain entry, but went completely unnoticed by the snoozing occupant. This mid-autumn weather was fairly typical for that time of year along the south shore of Lake Erie. "Football weather," Mahony would later describe it. Low gray clouds, a blustery wind and an occasional spit of frigid rain were the norm for the season. Even when the sun did appear, its brightness did little to warm the scene. Oblivious as he was to the foul weather, Mahony was equally unaware of the drama those same winds were helping to orchestrate, some six miles away on Lake Erie. Unaware as well was he that in just a few minutes he would exchange his warm bed for a cold and wet bench-seat, on board a Coast Guard motor lifeboat, tossing, out on the pitch-black lake.

Piercing his sleep like a jagged lance, the shrill ringing of the telephone shocked Mahony back into the conscious world. Being the City Editor for the Lorain Morning Journal, Mahony was prone to being disturbed by the telephone at odd times for all sorts of reasons, but this call was about to send him off on an adventure that he had never even considered. Clearing his senses as best he could, the groggy editor answered the phone. "There's a ship sinking out on the lake," the voice of a Coast Guard dispatcher informed him tersely, "we've got another boat leavin' here in about 20 minutes headed for the scene. If you're here, you can go." Before the brief conversation ended, the dispatcher forebodingly advised Mahony to "Put on somethin' heavy." Apparently Lake Erie was in a less than congenial mood. Still trying to orient himself from his grogginess, the newsman glanced at his clock. It was just after two a.m.

Dashing into threatening circumstance was nothing new to Jim Mahony. In his resume were assorted adventures as a war correspondent, less than a decade before that stormy night in 1950. Still fresh in his memory were the times spent wallowing through the fog of war, armed only with a pencil and reporter's pad. Starting his career as a sports writer in 1935, Mahony subsequently had been assigned war duties in North Africa and Southern Europe. Now, just five short years after V.J. day, with the conflict in Korea suddenly growing, the thoughts of combat journalism had doubtless started to pass through his mind, on more than one occasion. Consideration for his wife, Phyllis and son Martin would weigh heavily in any such embarkations, the reality being that if he could, he would rather be in Lorain. Such matters were for daylight pondering at his desk and far from his mind, as the city editor sped down Broadway to Erie Avenue and toward the Coast Guard station. He had thoughts only of giant floundering lakeboats and struggling crewmen thrashing among the whitecapped seas. If the Erie Avenue bridge was not opened for some passing lakeboat, the newsman could easily make it to the station, just to the lake side of the bridge. All the stoplights were in the flashing mode at this hour and there was no cop in sight—the reporter's foot was to the floor as he crossed the bridge and made the sharp left onto Alabama Avenue and past the city park to the Coast Guard station. Mahony would be the first journalist on the scene . . . what a scoop!

Arriving at the station well within the allotted 20 minutes, the eager city editor found a team of guardsmen hurriedly preparing to shove off onto a fitful Lake Erie. Theirs would be the third boat out to the scene, but that did not slow the efforts of the rescuers, the atmosphere was that of a major operation. Dressed in the heaviest garb he could seize when he scrambled from his home, Mahony expectantly took his place aboard the rescue vessel and was taken once again into peril, with pad and pencil.

Pointing into the absolute blackness of Lake Erie, the Coast Guard motorboat beat against the seas. The winds were gusty at about 18 miles per hour and had kicked up a respectable chop out of the northwest, that sent frigid spray flying as the rescue boat met each wave. After what seemed like far too long to make the two mile run onto the lake, the third rescue team and their journalist reached the scene. Searchlights and flashlights darted about the whitecaps illuminating a bit of flotsam here and there, but there was little to see. The word was that several castaways had been plucked from the water, one of which was Elmer Norwich. "We drank plenty of Lake Erie water." Norwich joked, from pure relief. But there were many questions to be asked, as the rescue craft bobbed about the scene. Was this all of the crew? Were there still men in the water out there somewhere? And there were the "hows" and "whys" accompanying the loss of any vessel. What was known for sure out on the lake that night was the "who" of the wreck. It was the sandsucker JOHN M. McKERCHEY.

Utilitarian would be the word for the hull being raised on the construction ways of the Great Lakes Engineering Works at Ecorse, Michigan, during the winter of 1906. Christened JOHN M. McKERCHEY, the steamer was launched promptly at three o'clock on the afternoon of the 19th day of May that same year. Amid the bedlam of shipbuilding activity that was the norm at the G.L.E.W. in that era, the launching of a 169 foot steel sandboat drew little fanfare, but the truth was that the McKERCHEY was the first lakeboat specifically designed to carry lumber and coal, in addition to her sand hauling duties. That was the intention of her owner and namesake, construction baron John M. McKerchey.

Like most vessels in the sand trade, the McKERCHEY was of modest size and minimal power, since her duties would largely keep her along the rivers or close to port at any one time. With her humble length, the boat sported a 37 foot beam and an 11 foot draft, all that would be needed to perform her chores. Down in the engine room, a single Scotch boiler measuring 11 feet by 11 and one half feet provided steam to a Steeple Compound engine having 11 and 23 inch diameter cylinders, each with a 14 inch stroke. The whole works combined to propel the McKERCHEY with a paltry 350 horse power. To say that the boat would soon fade into the crowd of larger and more powerful vessels of the day, would be an understatement.

Rare would be the times when the McKERCHEY would carry cargos other than sand, in the years that followed her launching. Sandboats have always been an underrated but essential part of the construction and steel industry. Their cargos are used to produce everything from molds for molten metals to concrete for roads and buildings. The toil of the sandsucker is to sail out to the sand bars that make up some of the shallow parts of the lakes, drop a large dredge-like pipe to the bottom and through the use of hydraulic pumps, pull the sand and water mixture aboard. As any kid at the beach with a bucket will tell you, sand and water are a liquid compound, but the sand quickly settles into a very stable mass at the bottom, and the water is easily drained off. Such is the way that a sandsucker works. The sand and water mixture is pumped into the cargo hold and the water simply drains over the side via the scuppers. When there is no more room for water, all that remains is a heap of tightly-packed sand. Interestingly, sandboats do not have hatch covers or even hatches. Their holds are completely open, because the cargo, once settled, resists intrusion by water. With no need for hatches, the hold is easily accessible to unloading equipment which simply drops in and scoops out the load. All this made the McKERCHEY a handy boat to her owners, and a profitable working place for her crews.

In 1912 the McKERCHEY's operation was taken over by the C.H. Little Company, and three years later she was sold to the United Fuel and Supply Company, both of Detroit. Finally, she was sold for the last time in 1923. Her last owners were the Kelley Island Lime and Transport Company, and they employed the little boat almost exclusively on western Lake Erie. By 1929, Kelley Island Lime and Transport Company, or "KILT," as they were commonly known, decided to take steps to modernize the McKERCHEY. To facilitate self-unloading, a derrick with a 75 foot boom and clamshell bucket was mounted, with a tripod support, on the fo'c'sle. The boat was given a new pilothouse atop a Texas cabin at the bow, instead of its former place atop the stern quarters. Now, she had many of the lines of her larger contemporaries on the Great Lakes.

By 1950, the McKERCHEY had changed little from her 1929 re-fit, aside from the fact she had carried countless yards of Lake Erie's bottom into port, 700 to 1000 tons at a time. At six o'clock on the evening of Sunday, October 15th, she had just finished unloading another burden of sand for the KILT dock at the foot of the Erie Avenue bridge, directly across the Black River from the Coast Guard station. Now devoid of cargo, the little steamer was plowing outbound from the harbor of Lorain, clearing at half past the hour. In command on this typical autumn evening, was Captain Horace Johnson, whose 250 pounds seemed to fill the tiny pilothouse. In truth, the hefty master seemed to have difficulty negotiating the narrow pilothouse door which, caused occasional snickering from various wheelsmen, watchmen and mates. Such breaches of authority were not a problem aboard the McKERCHEY, because she was a working class vessel and carried no pretense of belonging to any kind of formality-strapped stylish fleet. Her crew wore the same attire as their counterparts who worked in the factories and steel mills ashore, so someone not willing to get their hands dirty had best not sign aboard a boat like the McKERCHEY. It was okay to snicker and shout and swear, for such were the ways of a working class lakeboat.

After making the six mile northwest tramp to the pumping grounds, the McKERCHEY's crew went to work and in no time a flood of liquid sand was inundating her hold. All about the vessel, the normal activities of a "workin' boat" went on, with no regard to the clamor of loading. By midnight, the little sand sucker had taken on nearly all of the 700 tons of sand she was commissioned to haul back to Lorain, and preparations to head back were underway. Starting his midnight to four a.m. watch in the engine room was fireman Chris Timmerman. In a short while, the pilothouse would ring for the engine and he would go to work. Unlike his fellow firemen on the big oreboats, Timmerman's boat would be dockside in an hour, and the majority of his watch would be spent in keeping steam up for unloading. Supervising the engine equipment on the midnight to four would be 51 year old engineer Ora Harris—he and Timmerman normally stood watch together. Going off watch and heading toward the galley coffee pot was oiler Percy R. Ward. His shift ended at midnight and he had until eight o'clock the following morning before he would have to appear in the engine room. As far as the crew were concerned, all was routine aboard the McKERCHEY.

Foul weather played in her wires as the diminutive laker finished loading and turned toward the lights of Lorain. But the conditions were not so rough that they would have given anyone aboard concern, the winds were gusty, but the seas were just rude whitecaps. As Captain Johnson ordered the sandboat brought around, her heels were to the winds, and seas allowing little more than spray to board the decks. Another 700 tons of Lake Erie's bottom were on the way toward industrial use. Oiler Percy Ward headed toward his room and he stopped at crane operator Jim Lange's door to wake him, and tell him to prepare for unloading. Lorain was a pair of pants and a cup of coffee away and quick turn arounds were the way of a sandsucker.

Before half past one o'clock Monday morning, Captain Johnson noticed that something about the McKERCHEY's deck and the way it was rolling beneath his feet was not right. Checking her trim needle carefully, he found his senses were correct, the McKERCHEY had developed a starboard list. To find the problem, the sandboat's master dispatched William Gang to go below and find the source of the flooding, which was rapidly increasing the list. With his footsteps on the steel stairs echoing ahead of him, Gang headed for the forepeak. On the McKERCHEY the forepeak area was the space between the bow-plating and the collision bulkhead, or the lowermost portion of the bow. Reaching that area, Gang was startled to find water already aboard and more gushing in at a frightening rate. With all the speed his feet could manage, the shocked crewman reported back to the pilothouse. Rushing back to the forepeak a few moments later with Second Mate Louis Hasler, to confirm the source of the problem, Gang found the area blocked by 14 feet of water. In a heartbeat, they both knew the McKERCHEY was not going to make Lorain.

A single glance at the ashen-faced second mate, bursting back into the pilothouse, told Captain Johnson all he needed to know, and Hasler's frantic tugs at the whistle-pull told the rest of the crew. Over and over again, the second mate sounded four long blasts on the McKERCHEY's whistle as a signal of distress.

Captain Johnson grabbed the radio telephone and broadcast a distress signal of his own, one of much greater range than the boat's whistle. Aboard the Tomlinson ore-boat RUFUS P. RANNEY, Captain Elmer Auspsetter had been watching over the midnight quiet of his darkened pilothouse, when the radio suddenly shattered the tranquility. Hearing the McKERCHEY's plea, Captain Auspsetter ordered his boat headed in their direction at full ahead. Of more importance to the sandsucker's people, was the ship to shore radio station at Lorain. The operator there picked up the distress call, and in a second telephoned the Coast Guard station. Coast Guardsmen Richard Larsen, Floyd Hitchens and Jack Roux hustled aboard one of the station's motor lifeboats, and charged out toward the McKERCHEY.

With alarming swiftness, the tired little sandboat gave herself up to an enthusiastic Lake Erie. Down in the McKERCHEY's engine room, Harris and Timmerman had been unaware of just why the whistle was blowing, but were determined to stay at their stations. Their determination changed abruptly, when a deluge of water burst into the engine room from the starboard side, as the deck suddenly heeled over beneath their feet. They became far more committed to saving their skins, rather than tending to a lost cause. Both men bounded up the port side companion way, arriving topside just in time to join the crew in manning the lifeboat. The McKERCHEY was now well over on her beam end, and gave every indication that at any moment she would turn turtle—and head for the bottom.

Sprinting to the pilothouse, watchman Carl Reardon found Captain Johnson holding the boat's wheel, wearing a life belt. "Can I help, or steer, Cap?" he asked instinctively, as if there was anything a flesh-and-bone human could do to save the McKERCHEY. "She's going down," the stout master responded in a level tone, "you'd better hurry and get off." Instinctively once more, Reardon did as he was told. At that same moment Second Engineer Fordyce Beckwith had been holding the thin line, known as a "painter," that was keeping the water-born lifeboat near enough for the crew to board. They had been having a frightening time, trying to keep the yawl away from the propeller, and were somewhat preoccupied.

It was the last time on deck for everyone. The McKERCHEY suddenly rolled over and foundered, just 15 minutes short of Lorain. The deafening rumble of machinery tearing away from its mountings mixed with the roar of intruding water, as she cast her people into the bitter cold of Lake Erie. Reardon felt her going over, and leaped for his life—in a desperate attempt to clear the wreck. Beckwith felt the end coming and dove overboard. The suction of the foundering boat pulled at him with the frigid grip of stalking death, as he swam for all he was worth. At the last minute, Lake Erie decided that she would spare the thrashing sailor and released her pull, and in a few strokes the fellows on the lifeboat pulled him to safety. William Gang had no time to leap over the side, and was clobbered by the deck house as the boat capsized, fracturing his left shoulder. Somehow, he managed to surface and was plucked from the lake.

Shortly after the boat foundered, the Coast Guard began arriving on the scene, in an effort to sort out the ordeal. There was not much more that could be done, other than transporting the survivors to the station, and marking the wreck site a navigation hazard. By the time the RANNEY arrived on the scene, the whole event was long over, leaving her crew feeling as if they had missed something. This feeling was totally unfounded, considering how fast the sandboat went down. From the time the list of the McKERCHEY was realized until the sandsucker went over, less than 20 minutes had elapsed.

Sunrise on Monday morning exposed about two feet of the McKERCHEY's bottom above the lake surface. Apparently she was hung up, with the upper works snagged on the bottom 30 feet below. On shore, a head-count had shown that all but one of her crew had survived the wreck. Only Captain Johnson was missing. A circumstance that would no doubt invoke romantic talk of the captain going down with his ship. and other such nonsense. Speculation from the McKERCHEY's crew presented a far more plausible and far less glamorous explanation for the master's demise. Odds are that the portly captain, now burdened with the extra bulk of a life belt, had become wedged in the pilothouse door as the boat flipped over. And that is where his body was found the next day by Coast Guard and salvage divers.

Throughout the day Monday, Jim Mahony shuttled between the Coast Guard station, where the 14 unscratched crewmembers were, and St. Joseph Hospital, where the five injured crewmen ended up. It had been a long day for the city editor, cold and wet, but he had the scoop of a lifetime.

The McKERCHEY's wreck lay on Lake Erie's bottom for nearly a year, until the L.A. Wells Salvage company went after her. Using underwater acetylene torches, divers dismembered the old boat and sent her to the surface, piece by piece, by a crane and barge. No one ever figured out just why the boat suddenly started to leak. Apparently,

Seen here hard at work in the toils of the sand trade, the JOHN M. McKERCHEY sails another day in anonymity.

one or more of her rusty seams just opened up. Today, nothing of the little sandboat remains. There are a couple of ageing clippings from the Lorain Journal, stuck in a manila folder at the Great Lakes Historical Society in Vermillion, Ohio. On each clipping is a smiling photo of Jim Mahony, the newsman who got the scoop on everyone else, in the wee hours of a stormy night in October, 1950.

Busy Days for Operator Cooley

*E*ach summer thousands of tourists visit the 'city of locks' at Sault Saint Marie, Michigan. After climbing the observation platforms, they watch in amazement as the colossal steel lakeboats snail into the locks, and are effortlessly raised and lowered to the levels of Lake Superior and Lake Huron. The casual visitor has no concept of the extreme care and professionalism required to pass the lakers through the canal. It would take only a simple miscommunication or faulted judgement to unleash pandemonium and let slip the dogs of disaster. Such thoughts are not just speculation. It has happened, with locks smashed, vessels blockaded and the lake shipping industry thrown in an uproar. It is little wonder that the modern mariners and lockmen allow no room for carelessness, each and every time they approach the locks. History must not be allowed to repeat itself.

It is to our benefit to turn the clock back and stop at points in history, some near and some far, where we can observe the workings of the Soo locks, and the people who earned their living in relation to them.

Starting the hands of time spinning backward, our first stop is in an era near to our own. On the wintry afternoon of the seventh day of December, 1992 the 647 foot lakeboat J.L. MAUTHE beat her way into the lower St. Marys River, and out from under a hum-drum gale warning, that had been up for most of the last 24 hours. Fading in the distance, off the MAUTHE's stern to where the dark gray-blue sky meets the green-gray whitecapped lake, is

161

the downbound 730 foot oreboat MURRAY BAY of the Canada Steamship Line. The waves along the MAUTHE's course have been no larger than 12 feet at their worst, so the MURRAY BAY can probably expect better as the day wears on. Precisely as the Interlake Steamship Company's MAUTHE comes directly abeam of the De Tour Reef Light, the Second Mate lifts the boat's radio telephone receiver from its hook. Looking much like a 1950s telephone receiver, the hand unit has a trigger in the center and functions like a radio microphone.

"Calling Soo Control on 12, the J.L. Mauthe to Soo control" the second mate announces casually into the mouthpiece. A moment later, over a frequency of 156.6 MHz, the distant voice from the Soo crackles within the pilothouse with the standard short response, "J.L. Mauthe, Soo Control. . ."

"Yes, good afternoon, Soo Control" the mate promptly responds, "the J.L. Mauthe inbound at De Tour Reef Light our draft is 18 feet nine inches our destination is. . . ahhh . . . Superior, Wisconsin, and we're in ballast and I'm also aware of the radio guard and I will call upbound at Mud Lake junction buoy." Stunned for an instant, the controller at the Soo is not quite sure how to respond. The MAUTHE's mate has just anticipated and correctly answered every routine question that Soo Control is required to ask each upbound and downbound vessel, upon initial contact. Such is the way he addresses all of the radio controllers around the lakes, polite, professional, correct and all in one breath. A trademark of sorts.

Shortly after the MAUTHE glides silently past the snow-frosted village of De Tour, the mate again is on the radio. This time it is the side-band set to call WLC for the three o'clock report. A moment later the MAUTHE is in line to make her report to Interlake's Cleveland headquarters. Again the call is routine, but far more conversation-like than those on the VHF channels. Ahead, the downbound KINSMAN INDEPENDENT approaches. It is not unexpected, since her progress toward the MAUTHE was easily tracked by monitoring her cross-talk with Soo Control on the radio.

At a quarter of seven in the evening, the glowing amber lights of the Canadian and American Soo loom in the darkening distance. At Mission Point, Captain Bryon Petz picks up the MAUTHE's pilothouse radio-telephone, and makes the required report to Soo Control. A heart beat later, he switches over to channel 14 and contacts "WD31," the Lock Master, on 156.7 MHz. Tonight the big steamer will be taken up the MacArthur lock, and as the wheelsman, captain, deckhands, mates and engine crew ease the MAUTHE into the narrow lock, Sault Saint Marie drowses across Portage Avenue.

Two of the five locks at the Soo are regularly used in 1992, those being the MacArthur, or "Mac" lock and the Poe. Only 800 feet long, 80 feet wide and 32 feet in depth at the lower end, the Mac can accommodate fewer and fewer of the giant lakeboats. Most restrictive to the Mac is its depth. Most of the modern lakers could not pass with a summer load on board. Such is the case with the Davis and Sabin locks, which have only a 24 foot depth, as well as the Canadian lock at 18 feet. If anything should disable the giant Poe, the traffic at the Soo would grind to a near-halt. Many of the lakeboats now operating on the lakes are so large that they can use only the Poe, while others can use the Mac only when not fully loaded. The vast majority of boats that would be stuck behind a disabled Poe would be of the U.S. fleet and not Canadian, for the Yank fleet contains a greater majority of boats built for, or converted to, the big lock's dimensions.

Such speculation of possible snags in the flow of traffic through the Soo mattered little to those involved in the

163

operation of the J.L. MAUTHE, this December evening. In case the Poe was put out of service, she would be one of the few U.S. lakers able to still make the passage through the Mac. Inching, as if motionless, the MAUTHE's steel bow is about to be placed "up against" the lock's lower pier, without so much as a bump being felt. "Midships," the master casually orders the wheelsman. "Midships," he parrots back, out of habit."10 feet" sounds the mate's voice over the radio. "Which way's she goin' there, Tom?" the captain asks, but his own judgement answers his question before the wheelsman can respond, "Put about twenty left on her again Tom," the skipper answers himself over the wheelsman's response. "Put her hard left," he adds a moment later in a most casual tone. The control for the bow thruster pops and gives a resigned hiss, while the third mate's voice cracks over the radio again. "Four feet forward," he reports over his hand-held radio, "Three feet forward, two feet forward. . .one foot, and we're comin' up against." Without so much as a shudder, the bow of the massive freighter touches the wooden fender of the pier. "Back to 20." the skipper orders passively. Slinging the Engine chadburn for more power, the captain calls for "Hard right, 267." It is the rudder setting and course that will "bow-walk" the steamer along the pier and up to the entrance of the Mac lock. As the open end of the lock yawns ahead, the wheelsman starts to steer a precise heading that will take the boat into the lock. Below, on the lock wall, deckhands walk with the mooring lines, as if having the behemoth lakeboat on a leash. A careful balance of forward momentum, aided by the precise calls from the mates on deck, brings the boat into the narrow confines of the lock, like a finger into a glove. Another combination of reverse power and cables attached to the boat's winches bring her to a stop, the gates closing behind. When it all works out routinely, the captain quips to the wheelsman, "Did we ever do this before?" making fun of the fact that the two men, as well as the rest of the crew, have put lakeboats through the locks more times than they can recall. "Yep," the wheelsman responds sarcastically, "I think so."

On the crisp evening of December 7th, 1992 the J.L. MAUTHE slipped routinely through the Mac lock, with the aid of modern radios and advanced electronics. Ashore, the local residents squeak their shoes in the fresh snow, as they go about their lives, barely taking notice of the big lakeboats. It is rare that the oreboats stop at the Soo for anything more than putting their lines out at the lock wall, and picking up their mail, so the local community makes a large part of its annual income from sources other than the maritime industry. Fair weather tourism makes up a substantial portion of the locks-related income at the Soo, but in the off season, most of the gift shops are closed. Offering the most posh accommodations in upper Michigan with its total Great Lakes Maritime decor, the Ojibway Hotel is open, business being shifted from the "walk about" summertime tourists to those who worship winter's snow and the associated activities. Across the street from the Ojibway, the Mole Hole gift shop slumbers, as do all of the establishments along gift shop row, with the exception of the West Gate gift shop. Through its glowing windows, a lone employee sits cross-legged on the floor, fiddling with the inventory. Beyond the picture windows of the gift stores, the MAUTHE slips from the lock—and not a head is raised. Only a solitary boatnut in his car makes an attempt to drive to the fence at the upper end of the canal, to admire the giant steamer.

In near silence, the MAUTHE slinks up the broadening Saint Marys River toward Lake Superior, and a late-season grain cargo at the head of the lakes. Behind, she leaves the peacefully-sleeping cities of the locks, waiting for the next vessel maybe many hours away. Modern radio, radar, and computers are all things that have helped the big steamer get safely through the locks, but are easily overlooked. If we could stop everything this evening at the Soo, and turn the clocks back over 83 years, we would find the Soo a far different place—with a few significant hints of things to come.

Stopping our clock this time in the late autumn of 1909, we would find but three locks at the Soo. Where the MacArthur lock would later operate in modern times, the Weitzel lock functions. Opened in 1881, it is 515 feet long and 80 feet wide, but narrows at the gates to 60 feet. This width easily allowed wooden lakers of the 1800s to lock down four at a time in twos, side by side. Where the massive Poe lock of the late 1900's would be, the original Poe rests in 1909. Started in the same year that the Weitzel was opened, the early Poe measured 800 feet long, 100 feet wide and nearly 19 feet in depth. In keeping with the industrial revolution, the first Poe made the Weitzel lock obsolete the day it was opened in 1896. It too was designed to lock four of the largest steel oreboats of the era through in the same way as the Weitzel could the old wooden boats. The Poe was constructed where the first lock at the Soo, the State, or Harvey lock, had been since 1855. Interestingly, the only similarity between the Soo of the 1990s and the port of locks in 1909 would be the Canadian lock, unchanged.

At the foot of the locks, the Ojibway hotel is not yet in existence. Across the street there is no row of gift shops, but there is the stately Iroquois hotel, and the chandleries and shops that nourish the maritime industry. Directly across from the Ojibway Hotel's future site, where the Mole Hole would be in the 1990s, the Park Hotel stood in 1909. This massive wood-framed structure is four floors tall, and a block long, with a front resembling an old-west boarding house. In a single cluttered room on the hotel's ground floor, a new-fangled device and a single man, both about to get extremely busy, have been squirrelled away.

Wireless radio communications were in an embryonic state in 1909. The equipment consisted of bulky components, some made of wood, and a telegraph-like key that would spark a signal through space, toward whatever nearby set could receive it. On the lakes, this new gadget was more of a unique status symbol than anything, and only a select few of the largest and most "modern" of lakeboats carried a wireless. Although the Pere Marquette car ferries had been equipped with wirelesses as early as 1901, many of the semi-tyrannical masters of long-haul oreboats were still suspicious of the device. They considered it management's way of looking directly into their pilothouses and over their shoulders. Other companies simply could not afford the new-fangled device, or found it took up too much space on the boat. The few onshore stations that operated such equipment used it primarily in conjunction with regular telegraph paraphernalia, and the men that worked them gained near-celebrity status. Such was the case at the Park Hotel, where Operator J.F. Cooley kept control of the Soo's wireless station for the United Wireless Company.

Wednesday morning the 10th of November 1909 had been shaping up to be a fairly normal day at the Soo. Steaming down the Saint Marys River toward the locks, in the normal crowd of moving lakers, came the 497 foot submarine decker ISAAC L. ELLWOOD, followed closely by the 600 footer LE GRAND S. DE GRAFF. Captain Cummings was in charge of the ELLWOOD's pilothouse and Chief Engineer Floyd Lyons was overseeing the boat's machinery. The chief was having no easy time on this trip, since the ELLWOOD was running on just one of her two boilers, and giving her engineering staff endless headaches.

Ahead of the ELLWOOD the 484 foot steel oreboat FRANK J. HECKER was already in the Poe lock and had her lines secured at the far end. Aft of her the wooden schooner-barge MARY N. BOURKE had just been secured and behind her the lock's south gate was already closed. Snugly moored beside the HECKER was the 259 foot wooden steamer LYCOMING, the space behind her to be taken up by the schooner-barge SWEETHEART. The SWEETHEART was still waiting just above the lock, as the tug NOBLE maneuvered to fix a line aboard and pull her into the lock. Once in the lock, the north leaf of the gate would be closed and all four boats would be lowered to the Lake Huron level. Downbound above the locks in the wake of the DE GRAFF came the WILLIAM B. KERR, WILLIAM M. MILLS and WILLIAM G. MATHER. All these boats sported a 60 foot beam, allowing them only passage through the Poe. It was seven in the morning and already it was shaping up for a busy day at the locks.

Easing his boat "up against," Captain Cummings slid her bow along the wooden fender of the south pier. With hard over on the opposite wheel and the ELLWOOD's screw churning ahead slow, the captain "bow-walked" her to just above the east guard gates. Her rudder was brought back around and the turns checked, to snug her beam up easy on the pier. Normally that is where the big steamer would have waited for her turn in the Poe, but such a position was not good enough for Captain Cummings. Ever conscious of the few minutes more that it would take for the ELLWOOD to snail the boat length and a half to the gates of the lock after they were reopened, and ever conscious of the traffic bearing down behind him, the itchy master decided to move closer—now.

Figuring that about a boat length would get him close enough to save the desired time, Captain Cummings rang the steamer's chadburn to ahead slow, and waited for his boat to move. And move she did. In an unexpectedly short time, the ELLWOOD had all of the forward way that her master figured he would need to glide the extra distance. Apparently, a bit of current was running and was helping her along. Moving the chadburn back to the reverse signal, Captain Cummings waited, but the boat did not break her forward inertia. The little bell rang, and the brass handle moved to the correct position, but nothing happened. A moment later the captain was frantically slamming the chadburn to the reverse position repeatedly, simultaneously taking Chief Lyons' name in vain.

Meanwhile, down in the ELLWOOD's engine room, the chief was using an equal amount of nasty words. "I don't know what in blazes he wants me to do, with this kind of steam!" he barked with a resigned groan. The problem was that on only one boiler, the ELLWOOD's engine was far more sluggish than usual. It was going to take a little longer to bring the boat to a stop, and if there was any current in the water, that factor was about to become mighty important. With her screw digging in reverse, the boat began to slow, and Captain Cummings shouted down to put out lines to try to stop the boat. Standing on the open bridge atop the ELLWOOD's pilothouse, the harried master could only hold his breath, while the boat closed on the extended south gate with agonizing steadiness. He was at the mercy of the laws of physics.

Like a giant steel sea monster the big steamer inched ever closer to the gate, and, at 7:38 a.m., plowed directly into it. With a nauseating screech, the ELLWOOD's prow shoved and twisted the gate leaf several feet off its hinge— and came to a belated stop. Her screw still turning in reverse, the boat eased back away from the disabled lock, seemingly embarrassed by the accident. To the amazement of the rapidly gathering lockmen, the ELLWOOD just kept on backing until she was a good distance up the canal.

She stopped long enough for a hasty inspection of her bow by members of the crew, backed out of the waterway and headed over toward the Canadian side, as if to lock down there.

Apparently, Captain Cummings knew only too well that he had put the Poe out of commission for some time to come, not to mention the traffic jam that would result. Before the shock could wear off at the American locks, he was going to get his boat through the Canadian canal, and that is precisely what he did. After clearing the lock, the aggressive master pointed the boat's steering pole down-bound, and steamed for the lower lakes. Nothing—including a bombardment of questions from Canal Super-intendent Lewis C. Sabin concerning how and why his boat had just put the biggest lock on the lakes out of ser-vice—was going to cause him any more delays.

Radioman Cooley's wireless station suddenly burst into a flurry of commotion. Telegraphic bulletins and wireless reports must be exchanged, advising on the disabled Poe Lock. Vessels with 60 foot widths were unable to fit through the gates of the Weitzel Lock, or any part of the Canadian lock which, although 900 feet long, is but 60 feet wide. Making matters worse, many of the boats that were under 60 feet in beam were more than 500 feet long, not allowing them to transit the Weitzel Lock. This left only the Canadian canal to handle a majority of the traffic. A major blockade was about to develop, and keytapper Cooley found himself in a rapidly-growing pile of dispatches.

Standing at the west end of the Poe Lock, lockmen sporting brass-buttoned uniforms and caps that read "U.S. Canal," surrounded Superintendent Sabin as the group pondered the twisted gate. Quickly they were joined by hydraulic engineers, and an order of business devel-oped, for putting the lock back in service. First, the three boats already in the lock would have to be removed and sent down the Weitzel. A pontoon from the Canadian Soo would then be brought over and attached to the damaged gate. The 100 ton gate would have to be lifted off its hinges and replaced with the upper guard-gate, which was identical and would substitute well until the main gate was repaired or replaced. To the end of the season, the Poe would have to function without the added safety of the upper guard gates. This decided, the process of patching the damaged lock began . . . slowly.

To give an idea of the commotion caused by the ELL-WOOD's frolic, it took until 3:15 that afternoon before the three boats in the lock could clear the Soo downbound. The ELLWOOD's tussle with the gate leaf quickly invoked memories of a wild day just five months earlier, at the Canadian lock. It was June ninth, 1909 and the upper lock gates were opened to allow two downbound vessels, the passenger boat ASSINIBOIA and the 424 foot oreboat CRESCENT CITY, passage. In command of the CRESCENT CITY was the unflappable Captain Frank Rice, who had rescued the crew of the M.M. DRAKE in 1901. Already secured at the lower end of the lock, the ASSINIBOIA had her lines out and was merely waiting. The CRESCENT CITY, however, had no lines out and was just sticking her nose through the open gates. Below the lower gates, at the Lake Huron level, the 436 foot oreboat PERRY G. WALKER was approaching the pier. It was the WALKER's master's intent to ease up to the pier and put his lines out so as to wait for the lock to empty, the vessels to clear and then take his turn to be lifted the 20 odd feet to the Lake Superior level.

What followed was one of the oddest and most unexplained events in Great Lakes history. As the WALKER approached the position where her captain wished to begin stopping her, he rang the chadburn to "stop," then to "reverse." The boat, however, started ahead full.

Repeatedly ringing the engine telegraph to reverse, the WALKER's master did everything in his power to stop her. As if having a mind of its own the steel laker just charged ahead and slammed into the gates. Exploding from their hinges the lock gates released a cascade of water reminiscent of Noah. The 20 foot wall of water blasted over the WALKER's fo'c'sle and stopped her cold, but it was quite a different story for the boat's up in the lock. With the upper gates wide open there was nothing to stop the Saint Marys River as its full force grabbed the two steamers in the upper portion of the canal. Like the threads in Elvis' trousers the cables that the ASSINIBOIA had secured to the dock popped in rapid succession and the 346 foot passenger boat shot off akin to a log in a flume. Moreover, the CRESCENT CITY was sucked down stream like a keg in the rapids with the might of all of Lake Superior at her heels. As the ASSINIBOIA burst through the collapsed lower gates, she peened off of the WALKER with just a glancing impact and then proceeded to stumble into the lower river. Captain Rice's boat was not so lucky as her predecessor. Deeply burdened with a dense cargo of ore, the CRESCENT CITY dragged her bottom across the lower lock sill, nearly wrecking her keel. As she shot past the gates, her beam snagged on one of them, tearing another hole in the helpless vessel. The oreboat's unexpected momentum whisked her past the WALKER and ASSINIBOIA, and she staggered down the river, sinking in shallow water.

The whole ruckus caused a minor traffic jam at the Soo and put the Canadian lock out of service for a protracted period. Minimal, however, was the blockade of traffic, since the Poe was able to accommodate any sized vessel operating on the lakes. Delays were the result of having only two locks in service, rather than three. The repercussions were vastly different the following November, with the Poe being knocked out of service by the ELLWOOD. This time a large number of vessels, all of which were U.S. carriers, were just plain stuck above and below the Soo. By the following day some 50 portly oreboats were stranded above the Soo and nearly an equal number strung out below the locks.

Inside the Park Hotel, the wireless and telegraph were practically on the verge of a melt-down. For 24 hours straight the messages had streamed in, and Operator Cooley and his assistant were kept continually busy. The standard reply to the vessels and their owners was that the hopes were to have the Poe back in service by late Saturday night. The tug NOBLE had brought the pontoon over and the leaf was made watertight to give some buoyancy. Five feet of water was left within the leaf, to keep it upright after it was released. With the aid of the pontoon, it was planned to float it to the south pier for repairs over the winter.

By Monday afternoon, the wireless messages had changed considerably. A wicked November gale had swept in, and a snag had developed in removing the guard gate at the Poe Lock. A gudgeon pin on the upper hinge, holding the gate in place, was jammed and rusted. It had been months since the guard gate was last swung, and the corroded pin would have to be drilled out to free the hinge. The problem was that the gudgeon pin itself was made of nickel-coated hardened steel, and was much larger and tougher than any of the tools available to extract it. The only status of the Poe that Radioman Cooley was able to transmit was that nobody knew when the lock would again be open.

Many of the vessels log-jammed at the Soo were rapidly running out of provisions, and the Park Hotel's wireless was urgently taking orders for groceries. Boats anchored a distance from the locks were given the convenience of

With little effort or regret, the ISAAC L. ELLWOOD managed to tie up the Soo and Operator Coolie.

sending an emissary over to a wireless-equipped vessel to put in their orders. On Monday afternoon, two tons of meat and large quantities of other supplies were shuttled out to the fleet. A Canadian patrol boat, out to scout the blockaded fleet, was caught up in the gale and was rapidly being swamped. A wireless message to the Park Hotel was received by keytapper Cooley, who in turn wired the Great Lakes Towing Company. One of their tugs was dispatched at once to the scene, rescuing the patrol boat and its occupants. Between the happy Soo merchants and the thankful Canadian patrolmen, the wireless device was beginning to show its true usefulness, and Operator Cooley was becoming a short-term legend.

There was one message crumpled in Radioman Cooley's waste basket that seemed not to belong there. Scrawled on the pad was an urgent flash, reporting that the steamer "WOLVIN HOYT" had struck "Superior Reef," and had gone down Saturday night, taking all or most of her crew to their doom. "Superior Reef," was the long-fabled "pinnacle of doom," around which mariners had woven thousands of tales. According to the legend, the pinnacle of doom was an outcropping of rock jutting up from the depths of Lake Superior to within a few fathoms of the surface. Hidden in calm weather, the pinnacle was exposed only when the waves billowed in a strong blow. It was then exposed in the sea trough and waited like a fang to rip the bowels out of unsuspecting lakeboats, and hidden again when the waves subsided. This phantom spike of rock was located on the path between Thunder Bay, Ontario and the Soo in mid-lake—and had been blamed for many boats that had sailed away on Superior. By Monday, inquiries from Detroit were piling up at the Park Hotel, about the lost WOLVIN HOYT. All this was quite a nuisance to Operator Cooley, because there was no boat sailing the lakes named WOLVIN HOYT and, as of 1909, no pinnacle of doom had ever been charted. The wireless dispatch was a hoax. Some wireless operator out on the blockaded fleet had gotten bored and decided to entertain himself with a sick attempt at a joke, by inventing the WOLVIN HOYT . . . his very own ghost ship. In the days that followed, the hoaxer sank two more fictitious ore-boats. By that time, Cooley and everyone else were just ignoring the messages.

It is of interest that 20 years after these phantom reports of the supposedly mythical pinnacle of doom, the legend was found to exist. Just 20 miles north of the course between Thunder Bay and the Soo, there is a stiletto spike of rock that rises from a depth of more than 500 feet to just 21 feet below the surface, within the space of about three miles. Discovered in 1929, it was named Superior Shoal and is 40 miles from the nearest land. The

WOLVIN HOYT never did exist, other than within the prankster's mind of a bored wireless operator.

Five days after the Poe Lock had been knocked out of commission, under cover of darkness and nearly unnoticed, a curious event took place late Monday night. Unobtrusively, the ISAAC L. ELLWOOD slunk into the Weitzel lock, upbound. No doubt from one of the steamer's vantage points, Captain Cummings had a front row seat to observe the chaos that he had made. Under a glowing mass of yellowed work lamps, the lock engineers struggled with the jammed guard gate pin and, although there is no record of it, chances are that the work paused for a protracted period, while the ELLWOOD passed. Disdainful scowls and grumbles of blame were doubtless abundant—until the guilty steamer passed from sight, skulking up the St. Marys River.

For nearly five days, the lockmen had worked at the single unyielding gudgeon pin. The pivot won and the hydraulic engineers embarked on a new tactic. The bronze bushing surrounding the pin would be attacked with a drill, until enough had been removed for the pin to be wiggled loose. This operation alone took 36 hours, but the stubborn peg was at last removed. The gate was lifted with the pontoons and eased into the space vacated by the leaf damaged by the ELLWOOD. From the Park Hotel, Operator Cooley passed this encouraging information on to the blockaded fleet. The stations aboard the JAMES H. HOYT, WILPEN, WILLIAM B. DAVOCK and SIERRA received the wireless message and passed it on to those not wireless-equipped. There were more than 300 lakers piled up above the locks by now, the boats had log-jammed north of Point Louise. Their need for provisions multiplied as the fleet grew and meat and canned goods were being ordered by the railroad carload, so any news of progress was welcomed gleefully, by the lakeboats and Soo shopkeepers alike.

Seven days and 12 hours, to the minute, from the time that the ELLWOOD had impacted the leaf of the Poe, the steamer A.E. AMES passed downbound, through that same lock. At long last, the lake's largest lock was back in service—the blockade was broken. Unhappily for the largest lakers waiting above the locks, the water levels on lake Superior were at their lowest point since October of 1892. This meant double jeopardy for the big lakers since several were about an inch too deep to transit the Poe. They would be stuck above the locks for a few costly days more, until the water levels came back up.

Cranking our time machine back up to the present day, we can see a number of similarities between the blockade of November, 1909 and what might happen if some accident should befall the Poe lock of the 1990s. As of this writing, there are 16 lakers that can fit through no lock other than the Poe, plus another half dozen who can squeeze between the gates of the other American locks, but not carry anything resembling a normal load. Once again, the lakers have outgrown the locks. It is only a matter of time before someone makes a small error—and history repeats itself with another blockade. This illustrates the need at the Soo for another giant lock similar to the Poe, possibly constructed on the site where the unused Davis and Sabin locks slumber. But in this era of federal and state budget cutting, there probably will not be a new lock—until something happens to the Poe once again. When that day comes, we may look across the street from the Ojibway Hotel, and see the ghostly image of Operator Cooley, poised at a translucent desk with his telegraph key at the ready . . . waiting for the start of a busy day.

Three Sheets on
the Message-Board

*O*verlapping the November 1909 blockade at the Soo, and about to complicate wireless operator Cooley's workload, was the fierce gale that plowed across Lake Superior in the first hours of Monday the 15th. Lashing greater than 60 miles per hour, the winds brought a blinding snow that smothered the visibility of the luckless mariners on the lake and Saint Marys River. The towering seas and arctic temperatures only added to the dilemma, each sea slapping at the vessels forming ice on their hulls, decks and rigging. Without the benefit of radar, gyro compass, LORAN, Global Positioning Systems, or any other aid to navigation that the vesselmen of modern times have at their disposal, the mariners of 1909 were left to grope blindly through the storm, using compass and clock and seaman's instinct alone.

On Sunday afternoon, the day before the storm began, the skies and lake were calm along the northern shore of Superior. At the neighboring ports of Fort William and Port Arthur, Ontario, a score of lakeboats were in various stages of loading grain. As early as 1909, these two Canadian ports were sprawling meccas of grain distribution. Towering elevators filled the lakers waiting below with assorted grains, harvested from the western and central provinces. Most of the product was then hauled to the lower lakes, to feed the eastern Canadian cities. As iron ore was the backbone of the American Great Lakes fleet, grain was of a like importance to the Canadian Mariners. The problem is that the majority of grain is harvested in late summer, and winter's ice locks the lakes up tight by late December or early January. As a result, each year means a tremendous effort to move the grain across the lakes before navigation closes—regardless of the weather. This annual frenzy is commonly known as "the fall grain rush."

By six o'clock Sunday afternoon, the Algoma Central Line's three island canaler PALIKI had taken a full load of grain from one of the Fort William elevators, and was making her way toward Lake Superior. As the PALIKI was clearing the port, her master took note of the venerable steamer IONIC, loading at another elevator.

"There's an old-timer eh?" the PALIKI's master commented to the wheelsman, "That one's been around nearly as long as I can remember." Tapping at his barometer out of pure habit, the captain took casual estimate of the IONIC's loading progress. "Looks like he's got about six hours left under the chutes."

Having started her career back in 1872, the IONIC was currently hauling for the Northern Navigation Company of Collingwood, Ontario. This was a bit of a departure from her normal duties in the package freight runs, but it was standard policy for her owners to press their hulls into the grain rush each autumn. When she slid from the ways at Buffalo, New York's King Iron Works, the steamer was christened CUBA, and was one of what was considered to be the future in marine construction, the all iron plated hull. Her dimensions were 246 feet in length with 35 feet across her beam and 24 feet in depth, all considered monstrous by 1872 standards. In subsequent years, the boat's proportions were surpassed by many other lakers, simply through the normal process of lakeboat evolution. She was eventually sold Canadian and in 1906 was re-named

IONIC. By 1909 the vintage iron hulled lakeboat had been merged into the anonymity of the massive fleet of lakeboats, her only distinction being dubbed one of the "old-timers."

At the same time the PALIKI's skipper was pondering the old IONIC, another Canadian grain carrier was preparing to push out of Port Arthur with a load. Under the command of Captain Alexander Birnie, the nine year old steamer OTTAWA was hauling her cargo under the house flag of the Canadian Atlantic Transit Company of Montreal, Quebec. Certainly if the IONIC was among the first of the breed of iron hulls, the OTTAWA was one of the last. Assembled at the Bertram Engine Works at Toronto, Ontario, the OTTAWA's design had one purpose in mind, carrying bulk commodities through the Welland Canal and St.Lawrence Seaway. With the restrictive size of those locks in mind, the steamer was given the standard canaler dimensions of 253 feet in length, 43 feet in beam and 25 and one half feet in depth. Just why her builders chose to fashion her hull of iron, in an era when steel hulls were cheaper and more easily built, is unclear, but she was one of the last of her breed. On that deceptively calm night in 1909, Captain Birnie directed the OTTAWA's stalwart iron mass onto Lake Superior, their destination Lowertown, Ontario.

Through pure coincidence, Captain Birnie's son was nearby, sailing up the Saint Marys River as second mate on the wooden package steamer ROME. Constructed in 1879 under the supervision of Thomas Quayle at Cleveland, Ohio, the ROME was, like the IONIC, one of the old-timers. An arched package and passenger steamer, she was an elegant throw-back to the days when passengers were carried in quarters on the spar deck and package cargo loaded through side-ports into the hold below. By 1909 the ROME had been relegated to less glamorous toil, and as she made her way up the lower Saint Marys River, her hold was stuffed with 6000 barrels of powdered cement. The cargo was consigned to the Talbot Construction Company which intended to use it in the construction of another blast furnace at the Soo's Lake Superior Corporation. Moreover, the old boat was assigned two schooner-barges to tow at her heels, one being the elegant three masted schooner J.I. CASE.

As all these different lakers went about their respective chores, a vortex of destiny was about to envelop them into a stew of confusion and destruction. None aboard the IONIC, OTTAWA or ROME, had the slightest inkling that their boats would end up as pages on Operator Cooley's message board . . . at the Park Hotel.

In the first hours of Monday, the 15th day of November, 1909 Lake Superior let go an unexpected tantrum that caught nearly every mariner off guard. The winds leaped from a late season bluster to gale force, and with it a choking snowstorm. For most of three days, this late-season gagger assaulted the entire Lake Superior region, finally easing on Thursday. It did not take that long before evidence of the enormous lake's frenzy was uncovered.

Late Monday night, the Canadian Pacific Line's passenger steamer ASSINIBOIA eased her beam up against the Government Dock at the Canadian Soo. As her lines were being made secure, word was shouted down from the bridge-wing that the steamer had passed through a field of wreckage, on her way down to the Soo. Seen among the heaving seas were pieces of a steamer's cabin, chairs and two masts, silent affirmation that a vessel of some kind had met her doom. With the gale still blowing a blizzard, and the waves running high, it was impossible for the ASSINIBOIA's people to make any further investigation of the flotsam. The location of the debris, 20 odd miles east

The elderly IONIC went "overdue" in the same storm that claimed the OTTAWA.

southeast of Passage Island, was noted in the ASSINI-BOIA's log, and the big steamer beat her way onward to the Soo.

Quickly, the word spread around Sault Saint Marie that a steamer had gone down out on the lake. With their usual haste, the local media assumed that it was a down-bounder, and following an equally hasty head count of the boats blockaded above the locks, concluded that the only overdue boat was the elderly IONIC. Long before the newspapers could start rolling off the presses, word of mouth had spread the news of the IONIC's loss and the demise of her crew of 20, around the Soo. Telegraph messages were flashed about the lakes, expanding the story of the luck-less steamer. From his cubbyhole at the Soo's Park Hotel, Operator Cooley broadcast an inquiry to all the boats able to receive his wireless signal, asking for any information of

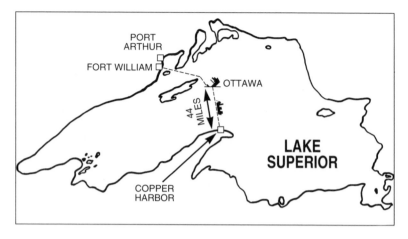

the IONIC. There were no replies. The following morning, the PALIKI arrived at the Canadian locks and left the information that they had last seen the IONIC still loading. Since the PALIKI had just arrived at the Soo, there was no real reason to presume the IONIC overdue, for she had to be behind the Algoma boat. This word naturally did little to quell the juicy scuttlebutt about the missing steamer and her lost crew.

As the first daylight of that Monday began to belatedly lighten the deep storm gray, the IONIC's counterpart, OTTAWA was engaged in a struggle with Superior that she would not win. Shortly after leaving Thunder Bay, the OTTAWA was overtaken by the gale and soon was being tossed upon giant seas. Before long, the cargo of grain began to slide about in her hold like dry loose sand. During the pre-dawn hours, the boat's crew worked feverishly with rake and shovel to keep the grain cargo trimmed. Sunken to their hips in the dry quicksand-like payload, the crewmen tossed the grain around the barn-sized hold, the whole scene rolling and pitching in insane angles. Lanterns could not be used to illuminate the hold as grain dust is nearly as volatile as gasoline fumes, so the work went on with a dim incandescent light bulb or two. It was a futile effort, for, no sooner would the vesselmen begin to work at a stray accumulation of grain than the boat would roll severely, and tons of wheat would cascade past them in the other direction. Yet they shoveled on, as if they could tranquilize the 1,344 ton steamer with their elbow-grease alone.

Complicating the OTTAWA's situation was the failure of her steering apparatus, thus hanging the canaler up in the sea trough. After a few hours of daylight, Captain Birnie finally came to the conclusion that his boat had but a short time to remain afloat. Waves were regularly boarding the stern, invading every opening, and the OTTAWA was now, not only listing, but down by her heels. The boat was just under two dozen miles below the eastern tip of Isle Royale, when the captain gave the order to lash the whistle-pull down, as a constant distress signal, take to the boats and abandon the OTTAWA to Lake Superior.

For any Great Lakes Maritime buff who has been told time and again that in a wild gale a vessel's lifeboats are only a psychological pacifier, because they cannot be launched nor afterward remain afloat, what happened to the crew on that deplorable night can be an example of why you can not believe all you are told about the lakes. Despite the mountainous seas and screaming wind, the OTTAWA's crew managed to swing one of her lifeboats over the side of the listing vessel, at the very height of the storm. Crammed to the gunnels with all 19 of the floundering steamer's crew, the lifeboat was lifted high on the hump of each wave. The icy crests leaped aboard, drenching the shivering occupants as they pulled clear of the sinking vessel. Captain Birnie's hand trembled against his will as he held his compass, and thick bursts of wet snow pelted the back of his neck. Over the continuous deafening moan of the OTTAWA's steam whistle, the captain directed

When the OTTAWA went down, she left her crew in a single lifeboat, in the middle of Lake Superior with a minimum of 44 miles to row to safety. Considering that the gale had just beaten down the big steamer, the odds were against her crew.

the crew to row southward, and pull with the wind for the Michigan coast some 44 miles away. Looking back through the storm the castaways saw the last moments of their boat—when it rolled over and was swallowed stern-first by Lake Superior . . . silencing her whistle.

Throughout the day the lake toyed with the tiny lifeboat and its benumbed occupants, like a cat playing with an insect. Surrounded only by the never ending waves and blinded by a veil of snow, those of the OTTAWA's crew at the oars pulled to stay alive, while the others bailed for the same purpose. It was probably this physical activity that kept them all from succumbing to the elements as the bitter cold wind and frigid water bit at their feet, faces and hands. Using his hand-held compass, Captain Birnie worked the tiller, guiding them ever southward while the horrible day dragged on. When darkness descended upon the stricken crew, a flashlight was used to read the compass and it seemed as if the Michigan shore would never be found. At 10 o'clock on Monday evening, about 12 hours after the OTTAWA had gone down, the lifeboat rowed thankfully into Copper Harbor, on the tip of the Keweenaw Peninsula. Astonished local residents eagerly took the shipwrecked crew into their homes, and all recovered from their ordeal. Obviously no one had ever told Captain Birnie that in a November gale, a laker's lifeboats are just a "psychological factor." Over the telegraph at the Park Hotel, Operator Cooley received the message of the OTTAWA's loss and the status of her crew. Routinely, he pinned the sheet to his message board and went about his duties.

By Tuesday, the combination of the blockade of vessels at the Soo and the whipping gale and blizzard, had given the steamer ROME and her consorts reason to tuck themselves snugly up to the Lime Island dock, in the lower Saint Marys River, to wait for one or both situations to clear. Alongside the ROME, the 320 foot steel passenger steamer MANITOBA was moored nearest to the open river, also waiting for the blockade and storm to clear. While the ROME and her barges sat straining at their mooring lines with each gust of wind, the little launch NAIDA came putting up alongside the steamer, and the ROME's watchman was beckoned to the rail. The weather was getting far too rough for the launch to proceed up river and her crew, Nelson Fisher and D.M. Seaman, both of Drummond Island, were transporting a seriously ill man, Andrew Wentworth, to the Soo hospital. Wentworth, also of Drummond Island, had become lost while deer hunting in the blizzard, and suffered a paralytic stroke, evidently caused by panic and exposure to the cold. They were rushing him to the hospital by the fastest means at their disposal- the launch. A few miles out of Drummond the two men realized the folly of their ways, as they were ingested by the snow hurricane, and decided to seek shelter. Darkness was quickly setting in and the ROME's lights appeared welcoming. After briefly explaining their plight, the two launchmen and their ill companion were immediately invited to stay the night aboard the steamer. After all, if there was one thing that the former passenger steamer had plenty of, it was spare rooms.

There was no way for Second Mate Birnie to know that his father's boat, the OTTAWA, had gone down, or even that his father had escaped unharmed. The ROME was not wireless-equipped and the bum-boats would not come down as far as Lime Island to sell the daily newspaper, especially in this weather. So, the oblivious second mate stood his watch, and then curled up in his comfortable bunk, like almost all of the ROME's crew. The thick oak timbers that made up her hull, and the wooden panels of her superstructure, were more than a match for keeping out the wind and snow, and the steam hissing through the radiators kept out the arctic cold.

Sharp shouts and the sound of heavy feet thundering past their door woke the two Drummond Islanders, but the fog that hung before their eyes was not caused by being awakened prematurely. It was smoke. Apparently the flames had sprouted in the bow and spread rapidly. The captain, whose cabin was the most forward, was the first to be awakened by the dense smoke. By the time the entire crew was mustered to combat the flames, the ROME was already a lost cause. The gale grabbed the flames, and the once proud steamer began to flare up like an old barn. The situation had gotten so bad that the MANITOBA cut loose and drifted away with the winds and current, her

For reasons perhaps never to be known, the ROME elected to go from steamer to bonfire. Thus ended a very productive career.

master not wanting to take time to re-start the engine. Before she peeled away from the burning ROME, two of the stricken steamer's crew had leaped to the MANITOBA's deck, and safety. The MANITOBA got up steam and stood under power a safe distance away, while the aged ROME incinerated. Like so many rats, the blazing steamer's crew went over the side and made shore on Lime Island. Both of the ROME's consort barges also cut loose and drifted down stream, eventually dropping their hooks above Drummond Island.

Watching in the knee-deep snow—some with shoes, some without—the ROME's crew felt the heat of her consumption radiating on their faces. Squeaking his way through the snow, Nelson Fisher made his way to the

ROME's dejected master. "We can take you fellows down to Drummond," he suggested meekly, "I think everyone will fit on the NAIDA." With the ROME still burning in the background, the remainder of her crew putted off to Drummond Island, in the same launch whose crew she had given shelter to the night before. Disembarking at the Drummond dock, the whole party was taken aboard the steamer STRATHCONA and shuttled to the Soo. On their way up, the ROME's former crew took one last look at their steamer, the storm winds fanning her flames.

At one o'clock Wednesday afternoon, wireless operator J.F. Cooley listened intently to the beeps and clicks that suddenly sprang from the set. The message was from the Shenango Furnace Company's 579 foot steel oreboat WILPEN, stating that they were passing Lime Island upbound. As he simultaneously deciphered and listened to the terse string of code, his pencil formed the message that the ROME was still burning, and the dock was afire, as well as a large stack of lumber piled there. After re-reading his copy carefully, Cooley tore the page off the pad and tacked it neatly on his message board, right by another page, with a bit of somewhat old but important information on it. Taken at half past seven that morning, the message was from the oreboat AUGUSTUS B. WOLVIN and reported passing the supposedly lost steamer IONIC, off Whitefish Point. At about half past nine o'clock that morning, the tardy IONIC locked through the Canadian Soo and pressed downbound for Tiftin, Ontario. Evidently she had been overtaken by the gale, and her master had chosen to run along the lee of the Canadian shore to the shelter of State Island, where several vessels reported seeing a boat similar to her sheltering. The 90 mile haul to shelter was a highly risky one, in the blizzard that came with the gale. The entire route is studded with islands and reefs that could reach out and snare a wayward laker in a heartbeat.

Doubtless, the IONIC's master needed every bit of his experience to bring his boat to the Soo.

Now, there were three different stories of three Canadian boats and their crews, tacked to Operator Cooley's board at the United wireless station. As time went by, the message sheets would be removed from the board, making way for messages of greater urgency. In the years that followed, the office itself would be removed, and in the decades that followed, the Park Hotel itself would vanish. What can never be removed is the story of the dauntless Canadians . . . and their battle with the November gale of 1909.

Sources

Whalebacks and Robber-Barons

REF; "Freshwater Whales," Wright

The American Lakes Series "Lake Superior," Nute

"Shipwrecks of the Lakes," Bowen

Correspondence with C. Patrick Labadie, Director, Canal Park Museum, Duluth, MN 12/1992

"A Pictorial History of the Great Lakes," Hatcher

"Duluth-Superior, World's largest Inland Port," Van Dusen

Ship Masters Association Directory, 1948

The Telescope March-April 1978 "The Life and Times of the Bessemer Fleet, part 1" Bugbee

"Namesakes 1900-1909," Greenwood

"Namesakes 1910-1911," Greenwood

A compiled synopsis of news articles involving the history of the steamer THOMAS WILSON, on file in the Canal Park Museum Library within the THOMAS WILSON folder, undated, author unknown.

"Duluth's ship canal and aerial bridge, how they came to be," Young

Letter from Kenneth Thro, Premier Great Lakes Historian and whaleback expert, 3/13/1993.

Meeting with Ralph Roberts, Premier Great Lakes Historian and collector, at his home 5/2/1993

Phone conversation with C. Patrick Labadie, Director, Canal Park Museum, Duluth, MN 9/13/1993

For more information, author recommends "In the Belly of a Whale," by Elmore Engman, (Wilson Wreck expert) although I obtained my copy after this chapter had been written.

Setting the Record Straight

REF;

Grand Rapids Daily Eagle, 10/20/1880

Chicago Inter Ocean, 10/19/1880

Bay City Evening Press, 10/14,19,20,21/1880

Detroit Free Press, 10/13,26/1880

South Haven Sentinel, 10/23/1880

TRADER's data sheet gotten from the vessel's folder at the Canal Park Museum, Duluth, MN

"Namesakes 1920-1929," Greenwood

The American Lakes Series "Lake Michigan," Quaife

The Telescope, Jan.-Feb. 1979, "Of Rabbits and Bulk Freighters," Bugbee

"A Pictorial History of the Great Lakes," Hatcher

"History of the Great Lakes," Mansfield

List of Merchant Vessels of the United States, 1874

Lake Underwriters Classification, 1871,1873,1875

"Ghost Ships of the Great Lakes," Boyer

"Shipwrecks of the Straits of Mackinac," Feltner

"Shipwreck!," Swayze

Lake Underwriters listing, 1879

Correspondence by mail with David Swayze, Great Lakes Author and Historian, 4/9,14/1993

A Cold Water Affair

REF;   Detroit Free Press, 7/23/1903

Harbor Beach Times, 7/24/1903

Bay City Tribune, 6/6/1902, 7/23/1903

Beeson's Marine Directory 1904

WAVERLY's Master Sheet, Institute for Great Lakes Research

"Namesakes 1900-1909," Greenwood

"Namesakes 1910-1919," Greenwood

"Namesakes 1920-1929," Greenwood

Ship Masters Association Directory, 1948

"Freshwater Whales," Wright

The American Lakes Series "Lake Huron," Landon

"Lake Superior Shipwrecks," Wolff

Phone conversation with David Trotter, Premier Research Diver, 7/1/1993

When the Winds Moan and the Snow Squalls

REF;   Oswego Daily Palladium 11/26,28,30/1921, 12/1/1921

Oswego Palladium-Times 9/28/1925

Inland Seas, Vol.48 No.2, Summer 1992, "Gus Hinckley-Lake Ontario Mariner," Palmer

The Telescope May-June 1981 "Oswego's Coal Docks," Palmer

The Telescope Sept.-Oct. 1986 "Franklin Phelps-Chaumont Shipbuilder," Palmer

"Great Lakes Ships We Remember Vol. I & II," Van der Linden

"Life on the Great Lakes, A wheelsman's story" Dutton

Michigan History Magazine Nov.-Dec. 1992 "Hauling Wind and Heaving Short, Language of the Lakemen," Pott

Phone conversation with Richard F. Palmer, Great Lakes Historian, 11/18/1992

Fire and Fog

REF;   Duluth Evening Herald, 6/22/1909

Bay City Tribune,6/9,12/1894, 6/22/1909

"Wreck of the THEW," Stan Stock, undated

Beeson's Marine Directory, 1910

THEW's master sheet, Institute for Great Lakes Research

Phone conversation with Bob Graham, Institute for Great Lakes Research, 7/7/1993

Phone conversation with Ruthann Beck, Thunder Bay Divers, 7/7/1993

Rudder at the End of the Road

REF;   "Namesakes II," Greenwood

"Namesakes 1900-1909," Greenwood

"Namesakes 1910-1911," Greenwood

"Namesakes, 1920-1929," Greenwood

"Locks and Ships," Soo Locks Boat Tours 1989

"Freshwater Whales," Wright

"Great Lakes Shipwrecks and Survivals," Ratigan

Sault Saint Marie News Record, 10/3,4,7/1901

Duluth Evening Herald, 10/3/1901

Bay City Tribune, 10/3/1901

Phone conversation with Tom Farnquist, Great Lakes Shipwreck Historical Society 3/1, 4/1993

File folder of the CRESCENT CITY at the Great Lakes Historical Society, Vermillion, OH

Shipwreck Journal, The Quarterly Journal of the Great Lakes Shipwreck Historical Society, Summer 1992

M.M. DRAKE's Master Sheet, Institute for Great Lakes Research

MICHIGAN's Master Sheet, Institute for Great Lakes Research

Phone conversation with John Kenn, Sault Saint Marie Historian, 3/31/1993

Harbormaster Wagstaff's Vindication

REF;   Bay city Tribune, 9/30/1883,
        11/13,14,15,16,17/1883

Huron Times, 11/8,15/1883, 6/23/1893

Inland Lloyds Vessel Register, 1892

"Namesakes 1900-1909," Greenwood

"Namesakes 1910-1911," Greenwood

"Namesakes, 1920-1929," Greenwood

"History of the Great Lakes" Mansfield

The MERRIMAC's Master Sheet, Institute for Great Lakes Research.

"Stormy Seas," Me

Signature of Misfortune

REF; The Evening News, Sault Saint Marie,
    11/6,7,9,10,12,14/1925

    Bay City Times Press, 11/7,10/1925

    Phone interview with Tom Singleton, eyewitness to the sinking of the J.L. CRANE, 4/6/1993.

    Phone conversation with Tom Farnquist, Great Lakes Shipwreck Historical Society 4/6/1993

    "The New Namesakes Of the Lakes," Greenwood

    "Namesakes II," Greenwood

    "Munising Shipwrecks" Stonehouse

    The Telescope March-April 1983 "504 feet. . .A Classic Design," Morken

    "Lake Superior Shipwrecks," Wolff

Captain Oliver's Extended Season

REF; Unidentified newspaper account of the STATE OF MICHIGAN's sinking provided by the Institute For Great Lakes Research

    "Great Lakes Ships We Remember" Vol.I, Van der Linden

    "A Pictorial History of the Great Lakes," Hatcher

    STATE OF MICHIGAN's Master Sheet, Institute for Great Lakes Research

    "Namesakes 1900-1909," Greenwood

    Beeson's Marine Directory 1902

    Phone conversation with Rod Danielson of Rod's Reef Dive Shop, 4/16/1993

    The American Lakes Series "Lake Michigan," Quaife

Mute Evidence

REF; Oswego Daily Palladium, 9/23,24,26/1919

"Namesakes 1910-1919," Greenwood

Beeson's Marine Directory 1920

Listing of shipwrecks local to Oswego, New York, Institute for Great Lakes Research

What a Scoop!

REF; Lorain Journal, 5/27/1984, 10/26/86

Bay City Times, 10/16/1950

"Namesakes II," Greenwood

"Great Lakes Ships We Remember" Vol.I, Van der Linden

Ship Masters Association Directory, 1948

File folder of the JOHN M. McKERCHEY at the Great Lakes Historical Society, Vermillion, OH 5/23/93

Telephone conversation with Jim Mahony, Lorain, OH, 5/23/1993 and written correspondence, 6/21/1993

Busy Days for Operator Cooley

REF; The Evening News, Sault Saint Marie, 11/10,11,12,15,16,17,18,19,20/1909

Ship Masters Association Directory, 1948

"The Great Lakes Car Ferries," Hilton

Phone conversation with John Kenn, Sault Saint Marie Historian, 4/2/1993

Letter from John Kenn, 4/13/1993

Phone conversation with Robert McLeod, Lock Master and Senior Hydraulic Engineer, Sault Falls Canal, 4/22/1993

"The New Namesakes Of the Lakes," Greenwood

"Namesakes II," Greenwood

"Namesakes 1900-1909," Greenwood

"Namesakes 1910-1919," Greenwood

"Namesakes 1920-1929," Greenwood

"Lake Superior's Shipwreck Coast," Stonehouse

"Locks and Ships," Soo Locks Boat Tours 1989

"Freshwater Whales," Wright

"Great Lakes Ships We Remember" Vol.I, Van der Linden

"A Pictorial History of the Great Lakes," Hatcher

"Went Missing," Stonehouse

Three Sheets on the Message-Board

REF; Sault Saint Marie Evening News, 11/16,17,18,19/1909

Beeson' Marine Directory, 1910

"Namesakes II," Greenwood

"Namesakes 1900-1909," Greenwood

"Namesakes 1910-1919," Greenwood

"Namesakes 1920-1929" Greenwood

"Lake Superior Shipwrecks," Wolff

"Freshwater Whales," Wright

"Memories Of The Lakes," Bowen

Index of Vessels

SKYLARK . . . 31
ANGUS SMITH . . . 43, 44
ANNIE L. SMITH . . . 13, 14, 18
PETER SMITH . . . 100, 104
SPOKANE . . . 5
STATE OF MICHIGAN . . . 127, 129, 130, 131, 132, 133, 134, 135
STRANGER . . . 100, 101
STRATHCONA . . . 190
SWEETHEART . . . 168
TACOMA . . . 100
W.P. THEW . . . 70, 71, 72, 73, 74, 75, 76, 77, 78
G.A. THOMLINSON . . . 118, 121
THREE BELLS . . . 31
TOLEDO . . . 100
TORRENT . . . 107
TRADER . . . 24, 25, 36, 37, 38
RICHARD TRIMBLE . . . 121
C.C. TRUMPFF . . . 104
TURRET COURT . . . 45, 46, 47, 48, 49
D. VANCE . . . 104
T.J. WAFFLE . . . 137, 138, 139, 140, 141, 142, 143, 144, 145, 146, 147
PERRY G. WALKER . . . 171, 172
WARD . . . 100
HOMER WARREN . . . 65
WAVERLY . . . 41, 42, 43, 44, 45, 46, 47, 48, 49, 50
DAVID A. WELLS . . . 25, 26, 36
PETER A.B. WIDNER . . . 117, 121
WILPEN . . . 176, 190
THOMAS WILSON . . . 4, 7, 8, 9, 10, 11, 12, 13, 14, 15, 16, 17, 18, 19, 20, 22
WISSAHECKON . . . 104
DELOS DE WOLFF . . . 31
AUGUSTUS B. WOLVIN . . . 190

Acknowledgements

With the creation of each text, the field of those who contribute grows. At times it is difficult to keep track of those who have given their time to bring a book into being. From the first notes scribbled into my little black notebook concerning the first story that goes into a book, until the publisher sends the finished product to the bookstores— two to three years will pass. Considering that a week is long enough for me to forget something, it is easy to see that I may overlook someone who aided in the development of this book. As best I can recall here is credit where credit is due.

Thanks must go out to the dedicated maritime historians who are so willing to allow an author access to their records and collections by direct contact or by long distance phone. At the Canal Park Museum in Duluth, gratitude to Pat Labadie and Kevin Guage as well as Don Van Nispen of Lake Superior Diver's supply and John Gidley of the museum ship METEOR at the city of Superior. Special thanks to Tom Farnquist for taking time from his busy schedule at the Whitefish Point museum to put up with my dozens of on the spot phone interrogations and to Sault Saint Marie historian John Kenn. Gratitude to Don Comtois, who finally has pushed himself into the age of the computer. Additionally great thanks to author and historian Dave Swayze. His "Stop the presses!!!" postcard saved me from a great embarrassment in the TRADER's story, as it was his digging that uncovered the single correction that described the boat's non-loss and had been overlooked for more than a century. I would say a word or two about Ralph Roberts, but then again, this whole darned book is dedicated to you Ralph . . . read the front. Thanks must be given to Bob Graham and Jay Martain, Dale Carrier, Dick Pfund, Richard Palmer, Larry Reich, Tom Rasbeck and finally Martha Long.

Also there are the dive-shop folks who I find are most willing to talk—in mid winter, that is. Bill and Ruthann Beck of Thunder Bay Divers, Rod Danielson of Rod's Reef in Ludington, Jim and Pat Stayer of the Great Lakes Shipwreck Exploration Group, Russ Golly of the Syracuse dive shop and lastly Dave Trotter who still does not trust me with the secret of new discoveries, no matter how many books I bribe him with.

Libraries and those who keep them in order are a source of great value to anyone who creates a book such as this. Proper thanks must be given to Carol Ferlito-Oswego Public Library, Mary McManman and the research staff of the Bay City Branch Library, Janus Storey of the Bayliss Library. All of these people and their terrific staffs have done more than they know to help in the development of this book.

Special thanks to the "eye-witnesses" who provided first-hand accounts of events that are beyond value. Jim Mahoney and Tom Singleton.

Finally, there are my close and patient friends and relatives, D.J. and Penny Story, "Bullet," "Binzo," and "Taz." Thanks to them as well as my Dad Walt, Mom Sue, Sisters Jeanine and Karen and my Brother Craig and all of those on that growing list of in-laws. Then there is my wife Teresa whose desire to participate in my lakeboat passion lead to her attempt to read one of my books. For some reason, before a like interest could develop in her she began to fall asleep. I relieved her of any further obligation toward my hobby in fear that she may slip into a coma. She does, however, appreciate my pecking at the keyboard, because she always knows exactly where I am when she's away on business—I'm somewhere in Great Lakes history, working on another story.

To all of these wonderful people and to anyone that I may have overlooked, I thank you.

About the Author

W. Wes Oleszewski was born in Saginaw Michigan in 1957 and grew up in the Tri-Cities area. His interest in the oreboats that sail the Great Lakes grew up with him, as they met along the Saginaw River. When he started the aviation career field in 1977, he was advised by a mentor pilot to find a diversion that would take him away from aviation in his off hours. The advice was sound and Wes took up Great Lakes maritime history as a hobby. This led to the development of a personal research library, and a fleet of some 40 miniature radio-controlled oreboats. In 1982 he joined the Great Lakes Maritime Institute, the Saginaw River Marine Historical Society in 1988 and subsequently the Great Lakes Historical Society, Great Lakes Shipwreck Historical Society, Institute for Great Lakes Research and he has woven close ties with the Great Lakes Shipwreck Exploration Group.

In 1985 while working at a Land and Seas gift shop in Saginaw, he found there were some relatively new books out on Great Lakes vessels, but for the most part they were just gatherings of data. Either that or the texts involved the facts about the same two dozen or so shipwrecks. It seemed as if no one was telling the tales anymore, and a year later he discovered the books in the local stores to be much the same. So Wes took it upon himself to tell the stories of the forgotten boats, and in 1986 began writing his first story with pen and legal pad. In 1987 he finished his first book and in 1990 it was published as "Stormy Seas, Triumphs and Tragedies of Great Lakes Ships." Before the first book hit the presses, he had start-

Author Wes Oleszewski gets a lesson in Lake Superior from Captain Byron Petz aboard the steamer J.L. MAUTHE, December 1992.

ed work on "Sounds of Disaster," his second text. By the time "Sounds of Disaster" was in the bookstores in 1993, Wes had finished and delivered to the publisher "Ice Water Museum," his third book. Before "Ice Water Museum" had made its 1994 appearance on the shelf, Wes was putting the final touches on this text, his fourth book to hit the shelf in as many years. As of this writing, work is under-way on his fifth book—he has enough material to write at least through book 15.

In his role as an author of Great Lakes maritime history, Wes makes frequent pilgrimages to various outlets around the lakes where his books are sold and the "Boat-nuts" gather. Often he can be found freely playing the part of "guest speaker" at local schools grades 1 through 12. He enjoys his research, and always makes himself available to sign his books, regardless of the supply on hand or location of the text.

A graduate of the Embry Riddle Aeronautical University, Wes earned a Bachelor of Science Degree in Aeronautical Science. He holds a multi-engine instrument commercial pilot's certificate and flight instructor certificate, as well as an Airline Transport Pilot's certificate.